More Praise for *Love 'Em or Lose 'Em*, Sixth Edition

"A passionate book about how to deal with the most vexing problem organizations now confront—attracting and retaining the best talent. With knowing wit and practical intelligence, Kaye and Jordan-Evans give us elegant solutions and engaging examples. Based on a solid foundation of broad-based research, *Love 'Em or Lose 'Em* will give you a sense of urgency, a renewed faith in your own leadership abilities, and delight that you took the time to read and use it."

—Jim Kouzes, coauthor of *The Leadership Challenge* and Dean's Executive Fellow of Leadership, Leavey School of Business, Santa Clara University

"This sixth edition is a strong shout out to the importance of using a diversity and inclusion lens as leaders practice effective engagement and retention strategies. Bev and Sharon say, 'Love 'em practices support engagement *and* inclusion.' Inclusion must be practiced in parallel with love 'em efforts or you risk losing key members of your diverse workforce. Read this book if you want tips for how to include, engage, and retain your talent."

—Julie O'Mara, Board Chair, The Centre for Global Inclusion

"It's no wonder this book has had a twenty-year life. The twenty-six practices that Bev and Sharon describe continue to give any leader at any level the how-tos of engagement and retention."

—Marshall Goldsmith, *New York Times* bestselling author of *Triggers*, *Mojo*, and *What Got You Here Won't Get You There*

"Our global strategy is based on recruiting and developing the best talent. Retaining and engaging that talent globally is crucial to every manager's business goals. *Love 'Em or Lose 'Em* is their playbook."

—J. Craig Mundy, Senior Vice President, Ingersoll Rand

"I'm a big fan of the 'stay interview' and its power; nothing speaks louder than a manager who genuinely cares. That's just one great idea from this latest edition of *Love 'Em or Lose 'Em*, which should be at every manager's fingertips!"

—Rebecca Ray, Executive Vice President, Human Capital, The Conference Board

"The biggest challenge facing organizations today is keeping their good people. *Love 'Em or Lose 'Em* can help you build a productive and healthy organization that people will not want to leave."

—Ken Blanchard, coauthor of *The One Minute Manager* and *The 3 Keys to Empowerment*

"Talent matters. Few dispute this truth. But keeping great talent continues to challenge many companies. This marvelous book offers specific tools and hundreds of examples of how to care for people. *Love 'Em or Lose 'Em* is the best treatise available on retaining talent."

—**Dave Ulrich, Professor, Ross School of Business, University of Michigan, and coauthor of *HR from the Outside In***

"The principles laid out in *Love 'Em or Lose 'Em* offer opportunity for all those committed to advancing true equity and inclusion in their businesses. The future of inclusive organizations lies in mitigating bias across talent management practices, and this book provides key practices to consider. Kudos to Bev Kaye and Sharon Jordan-Evans for timeless wisdom on retaining and engaging talent!"

—**Liji Thomas, Head of Diversity and Inclusion, Southern California Edison**

"You just have to love *Love 'Em or Lose 'Em*. This charming, clever, practical, and user-friendly book is a great desk-side coach for anyone who manages people."

—**Rosabeth Moss Kanter, Professor, Harvard Business School, and author of *Think outside the Building***

"Kaye and Jordan-Evans offer a user-friendly, practical guide that reflects the realities of diversity. *Love 'Em or Lose 'Em* challenges managers not to simply accept the loss of employees but rather embrace responsibility for the critical tasks of developing and retaining talent."

—**The late Dr. Roosevelt Thomas, Jr., author of *Redefining Diversity* and *Beyond Race and Gender***

LOVE 'EM
or LOSE 'EM

LOVE 'EM or LOSE 'EM

GETTING GOOD PEOPLE TO STAY

SIXTH EDITION

Beverly Kaye and
Sharon Jordan-Evans

Berrett-Koehler Publishers, Inc.

Berrett-Koehler Publishers, Inc.
1333 Broadway, Suite 1000, Oakland, CA 94612-1921
Tel: (510) 817-2277   Fax: (510) 817-2278   www.bkconnection.com

ORDERING INFORMATION
Quantity sales. Special discounts are available on quantity purchases by corporations, associations, and others. For details, contact the "Special Sales Department" at the Berrett-Koehler address above.

Individual sales. Berrett-Koehler publications are available through most bookstores. They can also be ordered directly from Berrett-Koehler: Tel: (800) 929-2929; Fax: (802) 864-7626; www.bkconnection.com.

Orders for college textbook / course adoption use. Please contact Berrett-Koehler: Tel: (800) 929-2929; Fax: (802) 864-7626.

Distributed to the US trade and internationally by Penguin Random House Publisher Services.

Berrett-Koehler and the BK logo are registered trademarks of Berrett-Koehler Publishers, Inc.

Printed in the United States of America.

Berrett-Koehler books are printed on long-lasting acid-free paper. When it is available, we choose paper that has been manufactured by environmentally responsible processes. These may include using trees grown in sustainable forests, incorporating recycled paper, minimizing chlorine in bleaching, or recycling the energy produced at the paper mill.

Library of Congress Cataloging-in-Publication Data
Names: Kaye, Beverly, 1943- author. | Jordan-Evans, Sharon, 1946- author.
Title: Love 'em or lose 'em : getting good people to stay / Beverly Kaye and Sharon Jordan-Evans.
Description: Sixth edition. | Oakland, CA : Berrett-Koehler Publishers, 2021. | Includes bibliographical references and index.
Identifiers: LCCN 2020045194 | ISBN 9781523089352 (PAPERBACK) | ISBN 9781523089369 (ADOBE PDF) | ISBN 9781523089376 (EPUB)
Subjects: LCSH: Employee retention. | Labor turnover.
Classification: LCC HF5549.5.R58 K39 2021 | DDC 658.3/14—dc23
LC record available at https://lccn.loc.gov/2020045194

SIXTH EDITION

27 26 25 24 23 22 21   10 9 8 7 6 5 4 3 2

Cover and interior design: Kim Scott, Bumpy Design
Composition: Bev Butterfield, Girl of the West
Copyediting: PeopleSpeak

To Barry and our newlywed daughters. Lindsey and Jill,
may you always do what you love and love what you do.
—Bev

To Mike, our four wonderful kids,
and six amazing grandkids.
Thank you for continually reminding me
that life is really all about lovin' 'em.
—Sharon

Contents

Introduction

A Proven Approach to Managing and Leading

Admit it, you *love* them—even if you don't use that word. They are your stars: your high-fliers and solid citizens alike. You cannot afford to lose them. They work remotely or on-site and they show up every day to do the work you need them to do. They are critical to your success, and they are the heart and soul of your organization.

So how will you keep them engaged? How will you get them to stay (both psychologically and physically) while others try to entice them away?

This book will help you do just that. We wrote it for you—a busy manager who is doing more with less and finding your talent to be your most prized commodity.

This book is for you if you manage people in a small company (less than 500 employees). Today those organizations employ nearly 50 percent of the US workforce.[1] And this book is for you if you manage in a large company. Why? Because we focus on what *you*, the individual manager, can do to engage and retain the talent on your team, not on what your company should be doing. (And we agree, senior leaders and HR professionals have important roles to play, as they create policies and practices that help build inclusive, engaging environments.)

Are You a Manager or a Leader?

We use the terms *manager* and *leader* interchangeably throughout the book. We count on you being both. Your talented people do too.

Anyone can be a leader and a manager. You will have to be both a leader and a manager in your work; choosing when to switch roles is the trick. Managers optimize the organization and its people to meet strategic goals. Leaders drag the organization and its people kicking and screaming into a strategic future.[2]

What You'll Find Here

Research-supported and full of easy-to-do recommendations, this book offers four key truths.

Truth 1: Engaging and Keeping Good People Is a Perennial Issue

Never before have companies relied so heavily on their human assets for their competitive advantage. You need your best people to stay, regardless of economic ups and downs. By *stay*, we mean that your talented people have not just checked in but are tuned in and turned on as well. They are engaged in the business of the business. Engagement and retention are two sides of the same coin. This book is about both.

Truth 2: The Manager Has Influence

Many managers claim no responsibility for employee engagement and retention. They believe retention is largely about money, perks, and benefits—areas where they have little control. We know that is not true. In addition to fair pay, people want challenging and meaningful work, recognition, and respect. And they want to be included, to feel part of the team. You can influence these factors. Senior leadership and organizational policies matter, but you have more power and influence than anyone else in the engagement and retention challenge.

Truth 3: Love 'Em Practices Support Engagement *and* Inclusion

The truth is your talented people cannot feel included if they are not engaged. And they can't be engaged without feeling like they belong. They feel included and are engaged when you show you care about their *growth and development*, demonstrate a *style* that breeds loyalty, and continue to build a *culture* that attracts and keeps talent. When your talented people feel a sense of belonging, they can truly bring their whole selves to work. Notice, respect, celebrate, and leverage the differences among them. Why? Because when they bring their unique perspectives and skills, your diverse workforce helps you and your organization survive and thrive in a highly competitive business environment.

Truth 4: Leadership Development 101 Demands Love 'Em Practices

Love 'em practices (A–Z) must become second nature to anyone who has direct reports. Most remember the oft-repeated quote from the McKinsey War for Talent research, "People don't leave companies, they leave managers."[3] Although all the 26 practices are common sense, they are not yet common practice. Organizations that hold managers accountable for turning knowledge about engagement and retention into action will come out ahead.

Love 'Em or Lose 'Em: The Message in the Title

Readers of our book (this is our sixth edition) have loved the title **Love 'Em or Lose 'Em: Getting Good People to Stay**. But it's not just a catchy title. The words drive to the heart of our message. Here's what we mean:

> **Love.** Some said the word *love* would not be accepted in the business world, but we couldn't find an alternative that stood for so much. Love 'em leaders genuinely care about their people. They appreciate, nurture, grow, recognize, challenge, understand, and respect them. And they believe this is the job of being a leader.

> **Lose.** You can lose people physically or psychologically. Loss is just as serious when talented people retire on the job as when they leave to join a competitor.

> **Good.** Consider your solid citizens, not just your high-potentials. Stars are people at any level who bring value to the organization.

> **Stay.** Encourage talented employees to stay with the enterprise (if not your own department)—for at least a little while longer. Talent will be the key differentiating factor in the competitive battle ahead.

You have more power and influence in the employee engagement and retention equation than anyone else. For your employees, you are the *face* of the organization. Engaged, highly productive employees help you, your team, and your organization excel.

Research Base

We delivered the love 'em message to managers worldwide, and we learned—*directly from them and from their employees*—what works and what doesn't. Over the past 20 years, we've asked over 18,000 people the question "What kept you—or what keeps you—in an organization for a while?" Our analysis of that data helped us form the original 26 practices and chapters A–Z.

We've built on that original research, meeting with managers from large and small companies around the world. With our team of facilitators, we've listened, consulted, provided training, and learned. We've also used data from exit interviews, focus groups, articles, journals, and books to update and ensure that every new edition includes the latest thinking about employee engagement.

Love 'Em or Lose 'Em Is . . .

Timely. Things change and every new edition reflects that change. We've updated stories, which came from colleagues, good friends, and leaders who read the book or attended one of the learning opportunities we offered. We also bring you the latest statistics and workplace views. In every previous edition of *Love 'Em*, we've highlighted tips for recognizing unconscious bias and becoming a more inclusive manager. This time we've expanded on that important topic. We look through an inclusion lens in some way in every chapter, and we offer countless practices, insights, and tips to help you better manage a diverse workforce.

Timeless. This book is evergreen. The love 'em practice will work as well in 2030 (we plan to be around!) as it did in 1999 (first edition). Through 20 years of workplace changes, *Love 'Em*'s engagement strategies hold true. Why? Because despite booms and busts, technology advances, increasing diversity, terrorist attacks, talent wars, layoffs, and a global pandemic, people want what they've always wanted. *Employees* want—and now expect—meaningful work, good bosses, recognition, and a chance to learn and grow. And *managers* want their amazing people to stay—for at least a little while longer.

Universal. The suggestions throughout the book should work equally well for large and small businesses, in India or in Idaho, with appropriate customization for cultural, language, generational, ethnic, or individual differences.

But What If Everything Changes?

You: We dealt with COVID-19 and its aftermath, and it felt like everything changed.

Us: It's true. Both immediately and long term, it seems that the coronavirus altered everything: aspects of how we live, work, raise our kids, care for our parents, travel, educate, celebrate, collaborate, and connect.

You: So then how does this book help me be a better manager in a dramatically altered situation?

Us: We've written six editions of this book amid economic booms and busts, talent shortages, and massive layoffs—and then, a global pandemic. How could the lessons be relevant in every one of these times? The lessons work because people basically want the same things, no matter the era or circumstances. This book tells you what those things are and how to deliver in your own creative, authentic way.

You: I'm a good manager. So should I just keep doing what I do?

Us: That depends. Are you listening more these days? Thinking more creatively about how your people can get what they really want and need? Especially in tough times, are you asking questions like "Are you okay?" "What can I do? What can we do to help?" If you say, "Yes," then keep doing what you're doing. If you say, "Not really," then take stock, care more, ask more, and really listen to your talented people. Collaborate with them to find solutions to their unique challenges.

Close the Gap between Knowing and Doing

As you read this book, you'll think, "I already knew this" or "I meant to do this." People say that knowledge is power. But not until knowledge turns into action is it power. Jeffrey Pfeffer and Robert Sutton literally wrote the book on this topic. They say, "Managers who turn knowledge into action avoid the 'smart talk trap.' Managers must use plans, analysis, meetings, and presentations to *inspire deeds*—not as substitutes for action."[4] This book helps you close the knowing-doing gap. We challenge you to do just that.

Get What You Need from This Book

We wrote *Love 'Em or Lose 'Em* to serve as a user's manual—a guide to help make your life easier, in the moment, every time. We wrote it because you make such an impact on the lives of your workforce. That's an awesome responsibility that deserves all the help and support it can get. Here are some tips on how to use this book:

★ Create and implement your own unique version of the love 'em practice.

★ Use this as your guide—as you would use Siri or Google Maps.

★ Return to it again and again.

★ Highlight what matters most to you.

★ Personally commit to implementing the key message of just one chapter. Start by reading Ask and Buck—then go anywhere you want.

The *Love 'Em or Lose 'Em* mindset and its 26 practices for engaging and retaining talent are not something you turn on and off, syncing to the latest economic blip and the corresponding concern about keeping talent. The approach works best when it's authentic and personal, when you clearly believe in it and demonstrate it daily in your actions with the people you want on your team.

Start with a Self-Test

We suggest you check out your beliefs about managing, engaging, and retaining others by completing a manager self-test called the

Retention/Engagement Index (REI). The results will direct you to chapters you need to read early.

Your perspectives and beliefs about managing others and the resulting actions you take can predict the likelihood that talented people will not only continue to work for you but bring their discretionary effort to work every day.

Evaluate your engagement beliefs and mindsets now by answering the questions in table I.1.

As you read each line, A–Z, ask yourself this question: *If truth be known, do I sometimes think this way? Answer: yes or no.*

Table I.1. Retention/Engagement Index

DO YOU . . .	YES/NO
A. assume that employees should and will tell you what they want from their work?	
B. believe that retention is a job for HR or compensation professionals?	
C. regard employees' careers as their business, not yours?	
D. take for granted that employees know you respect them and therefore you don't need to remind them?	
E. think employees should tell you if they are not feeling challenged in their work?	
F. expect employees to keep their personal lives personal?	
G. avoid discussing career options with employees, fearing that everyone wants to move up?	
H. hire primarily based on functional or technical skills?	
I. give information to employees on a need-to-know basis only?	
J. think you are here to get the job done and that employees don't have to like you?	
K. believe that fun is not a priority at work?	
L. fear that if you introduce employees to others in your network, they might be enticed away?	

DO YOU . . .	YES/NO
M.	feel that you don't have the skills or time to mentor?	
N.	have only a vague idea of what it costs to lose talented people?	
O.	tend to hoard good people instead of helping them seek other opportunities?	
P.	agree that we don't have the luxury of loving what we do?	
Q.	fail to question policies for the sake of your employees?	
R.	deem good work to be its own reward?	
S.	think that if you don't control the who, how, where, and when, the work won't be done right?	
T.	avoid giving negative or corrective feedback to your employees?	
U.	consider listening to be simply not your thing?	
V.	view employees' values as their own business and therefore seldom discuss them?	
W.	believe that employee wellness is the employee's concern?	
X.	think that generational differences are irrelevant in the workplace?	
Y.	believe that power should reside with the manager?	
Z.	maintain that employee engagement and retention are not as critical as other leadership skills?	

Look at your yeses and go first to those chapters in the book. This book exists to help you move from yes to no on every line of the self-test.

When your no answers increase, so do your talented employees' job satisfaction levels, motivation, and loyalty. When those go up, you all win.

Time to dive in.

CHAPTER ONE

Ask

WHY DO YOU STAY?

Ponder this: How will you know what everyone on your team really wants?

When do you think most leaders ask questions like "What can I do to keep you?"

You're right: they ask during the exit interview. At that point it's typically too late. The talented employee already has one foot out the door.

Have you ever wondered why we ask great questions in exit interviews but neglect to ask early enough to make a difference? Love 'em leaders do ask. They ask early and often, they listen carefully to the answers, and they collaborate with their talented people to help them get more of what they want, right where they are.

Conduct Stay Interviews

Two decades ago, we coined the term *stay interview* to describe a conversation that leaders need to have with the people they cannot afford to lose. It all started when we answered the call to help a Silicon Valley company increase the odds of holding on to key talent.

Leaders there had just formed a multidisciplinary team tasked with creating a company-wide software system upgrade. That task would take one to two years. The leaders learned that once team members in other companies had been trained for the task, they were quickly recruited (stolen) by consulting firms or competitors. In fact, the organizations who had trained the talent often lost two-thirds or more of those highly skilled people before the new system was in place.

The conversation:

Client: How can we ensure we don't lose these people? How do we protect our investment?

Us: Do you know what will keep them?

Client: Not really. We imagine it varies by individual.

Us: How about asking them what will keep them? And what might entice them away?

Client: Really? That sounds risky. But we'll give it a try.

The result:

When asked what might entice them away, nearly all team members said they would leave if their next assignment in the company was not as engaging or meaningful as the current one. The task was then clear. Learn what each person meant by *engaging* or *meaningful,* then help him or her find that ideal next position inside the organization. It worked. The client kept all but one team member. Stay interviews helped prevent the loss of key talent.

When we suggest asking employees why they stay or what would keep them, we hear, "You've got to be kidding," "Isn't that illegal?" or "What if they give me an answer I don't want to hear?" Managers dance around this core subject, usually for one of three reasons:

★ Some managers fear putting people on the spot or putting ideas into their heads (as if they never thought about leaving on their own).

★ Some managers are afraid they will be unable to do anything anyway, so why ask? They fear that the question will raise more dust than they can settle and may cause employees to expect answers and solutions that are out of the managers' hands.

★ Some managers say they don't have the time to have these critical one-on-one discussions with their talented people. There is an urgency to produce, leaving little time to listen, let alone ask. (If you don't have time for these discussions with the people who contribute to your success, where will you find the time to interview, select, orient, and train their replacements?)

Guessing Is Risky

What if you don't ask? What if you just keep trying to guess what Tara or Mike or Akina really wants? You will guess right sometimes. The year-end bonus might please them all. Money can inspire loyalty and commitment for the near term. But if the key to retaining Tara is to give her a chance to learn something new, whereas Mike wants to telecommute, how could you ever guess that? Ask—so you don't have to guess.

ALAS

A senior manager told us of an employee who was leaving his company. On her last day, the senior manager, who was upset at the loss, expressed his disappointment that she was leaving. He wished her well but said, "I wish there were something we could have done to keep you," assuming that her direct supervisor had asked what would make her stay. But the supervisor hadn't asked, and something could have been done. The employee said she would have stayed if she could have been more involved in some of the new task forces, as she felt the participation was vital to her goal of growing her career. It was a request that would have been easy to fill—if only he had known!

Asking has positive side effects. The person you ask will feel cared about, valued, and important. Many times asking leads to stronger loyalty and commitment to you and the organization. In other words, just asking the question is an effective engagement and retention strategy.

How and When to Ask

How and when do you bring up this topic? How can you increase the odds of getting honest input from your employees? There is no single way or time to ask. It could happen during a developmental or career discussion with your employees. (You do hold those, don't you?) Or you might schedule a meeting with your valued employees for the express purpose of finding out what will keep them. One manager sent an invitation to give his key people some time to think and to prepare for the conversation.

Regardless of when you start this dialogue, remember to set the context by telling your employees how critical they are to you and your team and how important it is to you that they stay. Then find out what will keep them. Listen carefully to their responses.

He Dared to Ask

Charlie set up a meeting with his plant manager, Ken, for Monday morning. After some brief conversation about their weekend activities, Charlie said, "Ken, you are critical to me and to this organization. I'm not sure I've told you that directly or often enough. But you are. I can't imagine losing you. So I'd like to know what will keep you here—and what might entice you away."

Ken was a bit taken aback—but felt flattered. He thought for a moment and then said, "You know, I aspire to move up in the organization at some point, and I'd love to have some exposure to the senior team. I'd like to see how they operate, and frankly I'd like them to get to know me too." Charlie responded, "I could take you with me to some senior staff meetings. Would that be a start?" Ken said, "That would be great."

Charlie delivered on Ken's request one week later.

What If—

What If You Can't Give What They Want?

Most managers don't ask because they fear one of two responses: a request for a raise or a request for a promotion. They might not be able to deliver on those kinds of requests. Then what?

The next time a talented employee asks for something you think you might not be able to give, respond by using these four steps:

1. Restate how much you value the employee.
2. Tell the truth about the obstacles you face in granting the requests.
3. Show you care enough to look into the request and to stand up for the employee.
4. Ask, "What else?"

Here's how the discussion between Charlie and Ken could have gone if Ken had asked for a raise.

Following Charlie's question about what will keep him, Ken replied immediately, "A 20 percent raise will do it!" Now, some managers will say things like "Are you kidding? You're already at the top of your pay range." That response shuts down the dialogue and makes a key employee feel less than key. Charlie was ready for this possibility though. Here is how he could have responded to Ken's request for a raise, using the four-step process.

1. "You are worth that and more to me."
2. "I'd love to say yes, but I will need to investigate the possibility. I'm honestly not sure what I can do immediately, given some recent budget cuts."
3. "But I hear your request. I'll talk with my manager and get back to you by next Friday with some answers and a possible timeline for a raise."
4. "Meanwhile, Ken, what else matters to you? What else are you hoping for?"

Ken might have responded with his interest in getting to know the senior team—and Charlie was ready to act on that one immediately.

Research shows clearly that people want more from work than just a paycheck. When you ask the question "What else?" we guarantee there will be at least one thing your talented employee wants that you can give. Remember to listen actively as your employees talk about what will keep them on your team or in your organization.

What If You Ask What They Want and They Say, "I Don't Know"?

Remember that this is not an interrogation—it's a conversation, and hopefully one in an ongoing series of conversations. It's okay not to know. Some people will be surprised by your questioning and need some time to think about it. Let them think, schedule another meeting, and set the stage for an ongoing dialogue about your employees' wants, needs, and career goals. Engaging and keeping your talent is a process, not an event.

A psychologist shared this tip with us: "When you ask a question and the answer is 'I don't know,' you can say, 'If you did know . . .' and they will answer you!" Like this:

Boss: What would you like to be doing five years from now?

Julian: I don't know.

Boss: If you did know?

Julian: Oh, if I did know, I'd probably be managing a team and . . .

What If They Don't Trust You Enough to Answer Honestly?

Discussions like these build trust. Ironically, discussions like these require trust. If your employees are afraid to answer your questions for any reason, you may need to build a trusting relationship with them before you can expect honest, heartfelt responses. Try to discover why trust is missing in the relationship, and purposely act in trust-building ways. Seek help from colleagues, human resource professionals, or coaches.

What If They Question Your Motivation or Smile and Say, "What Book Have You Just Read?"

Be honest. If you're not in the habit of having dialogues like these, it could feel strange—for you and perhaps for them. Tell them you did read a book or attend a course about engaging talent, and you did it because they matter to you. Tell them you honestly want to hear their answers and you want to partner with them to help them get what they want and need. You might even choose to admit that the love 'em approach sometimes feels awkward, even uncomfortable (like a new pair of shoes). That "name it to claim it" forthright action can be just what's needed to build trust with the talent you hope will stay and play on your team.

Why Most Say They Stay

Think back to a time you stayed "for a while" in an organization. For some of you, "a while" is 2 years and for others it's 20. Why did you stay? What kept you? We've asked over 18,000 people that question. Our findings confirm what many others have learned about the most common reasons employees remain at a company (and what will help retain them). The items recur throughout every industry and at every level. The differences among functions, levels, genders, geographic regions, and ages are minor. Here are the top 13 responses listed in order of frequency of response.

1. Exciting, challenging, or meaningful work
2. Supportive management/good boss
3. Being recognized, valued, and respected
4. Career growth, learning, and development
5. Flexible work environment (allowing for a life outside of work)
6. Fair pay
7. Job location
8. Job security and stability
9. Pride in the organization, its mission, or its product
10. Working with great coworkers or clients
11. Fun, enjoyable work environment
12. Good benefits
13. Loyalty and commitment to coworkers or boss

How did your answer compare to the list? And what about your employees? Find out what truly matters to them by asking. Then create customized, innovative approaches to retaining your talent.

Is It Money or Meaning?

Both money *and* meaning are important. Some of you immediately noticed the fact that fair pay lands in sixth place on this list. Here is what we know about pay. If employees see compensation as noncompetitive, unfair, or simply insufficient to sustain life, their dissatisfaction levels will go up. Your talented people will become vulnerable to talent theft or will begin looking around for something better, especially in a favorable job market. But here's the rub. While it can be a huge dissatisfier if inadequate, even fair pay won't keep people who are unhappy in other key areas.

So if your talented people do not find meaning in the work they do, if they don't feel challenged or developed or cared about, a big paycheck will not keep them for long. Researchers over time have found this to be true. Frederick Herzberg and colleagues found in the 1950s that pay is a "hygiene factor"[1]—make sure it's there or its absence will be noticed! So do what you can as a manager to influence your organization's compensation programs. Be sure they are competitive and fair—then focus on what else you can do to keep your talent.

Does Asking Work for Everyone?

Asking works for everyone, but how you ask might vary. How do differences play out in this crucial, foundational engagement strategy— the stay interview? We asked colleagues, book reviewers, and clients around the globe, and here is what we heard:

★ The majority said, "It will work *here* just as well as in the United States."

★ One colleague said, "Barriers to asking in Asia are magnified because the culture demands respect for elders and leaders. Even if asked, most employees do not feel free to share issues that may reflect negatively on their boss."

★ An executive said, "I appreciate a heads-up and time to prepare for almost every important meeting. My boss knows that about me, and he always lets me know in advance that we'll be having a stay interview conversation in our next one-on-one."

★ A consultant reported, "In more hierarchical cultures like that of Japan and Korea, asking questions is not traditionally encouraged. If the boss were to say, 'What do you think?' the subordinate would say, 'Yes.'"

If you manage others in a culture where asking is not accepted or recommended, you'll need to find a work-around. Some managers have used anonymous surveys or tasked someone else with the asking. However you seek to learn about what your talented employees really want, it is crucial that you do gain that information.

> **→ TRY THIS**
>
> ★ Look back at the list of reasons people stay and ask yourself which of these you can influence.
>
> ★ Check all those that you believe are largely within your control. If our hunch is correct, you will find that you can influence many more than you may have thought.

Beyond "Why Do You Stay?"

For a decade now, we've collected managers' favorite stay interview questions. Here are the top 11, in no particular order.

★ What one change in your current role would make you consider staying in this job?

★ If you had a magic wand, what would be the one thing you would change about this department, team, organization?

★ As your manager, what could I do a little more of or a little less of?

★ If you had to go back to a position in your past and stay for an extended period of time, which one would it be and why?

★ What do you need to learn to work at your best?

★ What makes for a great day?

★ What can we do to make your job more satisfying?

★ What can we do to support your career goals?

★ Do you get enough recognition? How do you like to be recognized?

★ What do you want to learn this year?

★ In what ways do you feel valued and included by the team?

Let these ideas serve as catalysts for your own thinking. Create a list of your favorite questions. Ask them of your talented people. And ask again, listen carefully, and then *act*. Collaborate with your employees to find ways to fulfill their requests.

Note: Don't ask until you're ready to act!

If You Manage Managers

Are the managers *you* manage conducting stay interviews? If so, that's outstanding. If not, they need to start. Your job is to teach those you lead how to ask these crucial questions of their talent, how to prepare for employees' responses (including the tough requests), and then how to make something happen! Hold managers accountable for conducting stay interviews with all those they hope will stay on the team and in the enterprise. Ask them to share with you the personalized creative strategies they create with their talent. Better yet, bring your team of leaders together and have them share their experience with stay interviews. This joint sharing will spark great ideas.

BOTTOM LINE

Stop guessing what will keep your talent happy and on your team. Gather your courage and conduct stay interviews with the employees you want to keep, no matter their age, gender, or cultural background. Set aside time to start the dialogue. Don't guess and don't assume they all want the same thing (like pay or a promotion). Schedule another meeting if they need to think about it for a while.

To simply *ask* may be the most important strategy in this book, and it is foundational to all others. Not only will asking make your talented people feel valued, but their answers will provide the information you need to customize strategies to keep each of them. It doesn't matter so much where, when, or how you ask—just *ask*! Read *Hello Stay Interviews, Goodbye Talent Loss: A Manager's Playbook* for more information on this important topic.[2]

CHAPTER TWO

Buck

IT STOPS HERE

Ponder this: Who's really in charge of engaging and retaining your best people?

The following sign (figure 2.1) was on President Truman's White House office desk, and Truman popularized the now-familiar phrase. Every culture has its way of saying do not pass the buck. In Chinese it goes like this, 责无旁贷, which translates to "No shirking of responsibility."

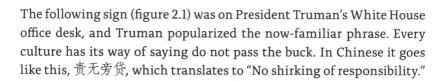

Figure 2.1. Truman's sign

When we ask supervisors and managers how to keep good people, many immediately respond, "With money." Research suggests that a majority of managers truly believe it's largely about the money. These managers place the responsibility for keeping key people squarely in the hands of senior management or the compensation department. They blame organizational policies or pay scales for the loss of talent. Or they point the finger at the competition or the location. It's always someone else's fault.

Well, the truth is, you matter most. If you are a manager at any level, a frontline supervisor, or a project leader, you actually have more power than anyone else to keep your best employees. Why? Because the factors that drive employee satisfaction, engagement, and commitment are largely within your control. And the factors that satisfy and engage employees are the ones that keep them on your team.

Those factors haven't changed much over the past 40 years. Many researchers who have studied retention agree on what engages or satisfies people and therefore influences them to stay: meaningful and challenging work, a chance to learn and grow, fair and competitive compensation, great coworkers, recognition, respect, and a good boss. Don't you want those things?

ALAS

There's nothing I can do about our brain drain. The competition is offering more money and better perks. We don't stand a chance.

—Manager, retail pharmacy

You *do* stand a chance. Your relationship with employees is key to their satisfaction and decisions to stay or leave. Consider this:

★ Research by Gallup found that managers account for 70 percent of the variance in employee engagement scores.[1]

★ Data from nearly 20,000 employees around the world showed that being treated with respect by their leaders was more important than recognition and appreciation, useful feedback, and even opportunities for learning. Those who felt respected were healthier, more focused, more likely to stay with their organization, and far more engaged.[2]

★ Globally, only 15 percent of employees are engaged at work. This means that 85 percent of employees either aren't engaged or, worse, are actively disengaged—ruining workplaces, societies, and general world productivity. It doesn't need to be that way. This problem is very fixable. Great frontline managers who are responsible for engaging teams have the most direct influence on engagement. Engagement is also about the people who manage the managers.[3]

★ More than 9 out of 10 employees are willing to trade a percentage of their lifetime earnings for greater meaning at work. Employees are more satisfied at work when the job feels meaningful. Building greater meaning is no longer a "nice to have." Frontline managers play a critical role in creating meaning and opportunities at work, coaching employees, and providing feedback for growth and performance improvement.[4]

★ Research by the authors (over 18,000 respondents) found that most retention factors are within managers' influence.

The evidence is clear. The buck stops with the manager. That reality is taking hold in organizations across the globe. Managers who think engagement and retention are somebody else's job need to think again.

In our exit interviews, for those who are honest, the major reason people leave is conflict with their manager. That needs to be dealt with, and those relationships need to be strengthened. Most managers do not see creating a retention culture as their responsibility. They do need to own this responsibility and be held accountable to create and maintain this culture.

—CEO, nonprofit firm in Singapore

You Matter More Than You Think

Be a love 'em manager. A good boss who cares about keeping good employees will help them find what they want from their workplace. We're not saying you carry this responsibility alone. Senior management and your organization's policies, systems, and culture have an impact on your ability to keep talented people. You may have human resource professionals who can help support your efforts. Even your employees have a role. See our book *Love It, Don't Leave It: 26 Ways to Get What You Want at Work.*[5]

Yet, because of what research tells us about why people leave their jobs and organizations, you still have the greatest influence (and responsibility) for keeping your talented employees. Because you do, it's important to realize employee engagement is not a one-and-done event. In fact, it is happening (or not) in the everyday interactions with the people on your team.

*Bosses matter to everyone they oversee, but they matter most
to those just beneath them in the pecking order: the people
they guide at close range, who constantly tangle with the boss's
virtues, foibles, and quirks. Whether you are the CEO of a
Fortune 500 company or the head chef at a restaurant, your
success depends on staying in tune with the people you interact
with most frequently and intensely. . . .*

*Linda Hudson, [former] CEO of BAE Systems, got this message
after becoming the first female president of General Dynamics.
After her first day on the job, a dozen women in her office
imitated how she tied her scarf. Hudson realized, "It really was
now about me and the context of setting the tone for the organization. That was a lesson I have never forgotten—that as a leader,
people are looking at you in a way that you could not have
imagined in other roles." Hudson added that such scrutiny and
the consequent responsibility is "something that I think about
virtually every day."* [6]

→ TRY THIS

★ Start with a conversation—a "stay interview." Learn about your
talented employees' goals and what they love (or don't love) about
their work. Don't stop with one chat. Talk (and listen!) daily, weekly,
and monthly. Develop a true relationship with every single person
you hope to keep on your team.

★ Look back on your day. Consider the interactions you had with your
employees. Did you model the behaviors of a love 'em manager? If
not, what might you need to do differently moving forward?

★ Hold "Alas Clinics"—opportunities to talk with others about talented
people who have left your team lately. Why did they go? What role
(if any) did you play in their leaving? How can you prevent more
unwanted turnover?

★ Think about who might be "loose in the saddle" (about ready to
leave you); talk with them *soon*, and collaborate with them to get
them more of what they want and need from you, from the team,
and from their jobs.

★ Go big picture. Ask yourself, "What kind of work environment do I want to create?" Then figure out what you need to do to make that vision come alive. Then—go do it!

B

So They Go

If employees leave, so what? Can't you just replace them? You might be able to replace your key people, but at what cost? Most retention experts agree that replacing key talent will cost you two times their annual salaries. And replacing "platinum" workers (those with specialized skills) will run four to five times their annual salary.

Even if you can afford to replace them, will you be able to find skilled replacements? The demographers and workforce pundits disagree. Will we be short millions of workers in the coming decades or have plenty to go around? The mitigating factors to talent shortages (globalization/offshoring, technology, automation, delayed retirement, immigration, changing attitudes about work) are so many and so complex that some feel a crystal ball would do as good a job as the experts when it comes to projecting the answer.

What we do know is this: the labor market is changing, and in many segments there aren't enough skilled workers to fill the jobs open today, let alone support a growing economy. In labor markets across the globe, many of our youngest workers assume that they will have multiple jobs, often staying not very long in each position. Managers go against that tide when seeking to retain young workers.

Notice what's happening in your own backyard. Do you have plenty of people, with exactly the right skills, to step in when you lose a key contributor? Or is there a current or pending talent shortage in your industry, geographic region, or job function? And, as you look at your team and consider what you'll need going forward, do you focus on skills ahead of gender, ethnicity, and other differences? Hopefully you do.

On the Line

Most of you are in charge of certain assets. You are held accountable for protecting those assets and for growing them. Today, your most critical assets are *people*, not property. A diverse group of outstanding people gives you and your organization a competitive advantage. Regardless of the job market, you no doubt want to hold on to your best.

Are you accountable for selecting and keeping talented people? We have heard of a CEO who charged $30,000 to a manager's operating budget because he needlessly lost a talented person. The buck really did stop there!

We're not suggesting that managers be punished when their people are promoted or move on to learn something new. Sometimes you love them and you still lose them, especially as they pursue their career dreams. But we do recommend that managers be held accountable for being *good managers* and for creating a retention culture where people feel included, motivated, cared about, and rewarded.

If You Manage Managers

Do you hold your managers accountable for the teams they lead? How? You've probably heard the maxim that busy people do what is *inspected*, not necessarily what is *expected*. You can expect—and should find ways to inspect—honest efforts to keep good people because those people build your business. And if the managers you manage fail to accept that the buck stops with them, *mentor* them, *coach* them, and, if necessary, *move* them out of management.

BOTTOM LINE

The retention buck really does stop with you. We are not ignoring the impact of senior management, organization policies, and individual employees' attitudes and actions. But we know you have great power to influence your talented employees' decisions about staying. Conduct stay interviews with every employee you hope to engage and keep on your team. Find out what these key people want and help them get it! Show that you care about them and their needs. Remember them. Notice them. Listen to them. Thank them. Love them or lose them.

CHAPTER THREE

Careers

SUPPORT GROWTH

Ponder this: How are you helping build their future?

At one time, employees waited for you (the manager) to tap them on the shoulder and let them know when they were ready for a promotion or an exciting new opportunity. Things have changed. Today, you still have an important role, but your employees actually *own* their careers—and they know that. They will leave if they can't find what they want right where they are.

Your job in the career equation is to lend support by providing perspective and having an ongoing dialogue that helps employees uncover and discover opportunities for growth and fulfillment. Yet far too many managers steer clear of career conversations. They worry about opening a Pandora's box, thereby starting a conversation they cannot entirely direct. If these leaders fail to have ongoing chats with their talented people, they stand a far greater chance of losing them—either physically or psychologically.

Which of the following attitudes or beliefs keep *you* from opening up this topic?

★ No one, let alone me, knows what the future holds.

★ It is just not the right time.

★ I'm not prepared.

★ I wouldn't know what to say.

★ We've just reorganized. It will be a while before anyone
knows anything about career possibilities.

★ I would never open something I couldn't close.

★ I don't know enough about what's outside my department to
   offer advice.

★ I don't want people blaming me if they don't get what they want.

★ Why should I help? Nobody ever helped me.

Your employees really want two-way conversations with you to talk about their abilities, choices, and ideas. They want you to listen. They may not expect you to have the answers, but they expect and really want to have the dialogue.

Talking to your employees about their careers does take time and may seem like a tough assignment. You may want to start with employees who have expressed concern about their careers or with employees who show signs of becoming disengaged from their work. Prioritize and take one step at a time.

The Business Case

What's in it for you to hold career conversations that help your talented employees more effectively manage their careers? Aside from the good feelings you might get, you'll no doubt increase the odds of their staying longer and producing more. Who wouldn't want that?

Retention research suggests that employees often leave because they have no idea of their value to the organization and can't envision a career happening there. Many report having never had candid conversations about their abilities and how they can leverage their strengths, develop new skills, and polish rough edges as they work toward their career goals.

Five steps you can take routinely will build your talent pipeline and support your employees' search for a good career fit:

Step 1: Know their talents.

Step 2: Offer your perspective.

Step 3: Discuss trends.

Step 4: Discover multiple options.

Step 5: Codesign an action plan.

Step 1: Know Their Talents

The primary objective of career conversations is to gather information that will tell you more about your employees. It is not always easy for them to talk about their skills, values, and interests. Some will think of it as bragging, or they'll fear appearing disloyal if they discuss career goals beyond the current job. Many managers in Asia report this to be a challenge—how to hold an honest career discussion, given cultural norms and values that support humility and loyalty.

Consider, too, diversity of cultures and customs as you prepare for these conversations. Something so simple as providing tea as well as coffee, and having options for cultures that do not use caffeine, is an eloquent gesture.

The ultimate goal is to ask questions about your employees' unique skills, interests, and values. The toughest part is to listen while they answer, as a diligent researcher or an archeologist on a dig would. Probe, inquire, and discover more.

→ TRY THIS

Ask these questions, and then probe each answer more deeply:

★ What makes you unique in this organization?

★ Tell me about one of your accomplishments that makes you particularly proud.

★ What are your most important work-related values? Which values are met and not met at work?

★ If you had to choose among working with people, data, things, or ideas, which mixture would be most satisfying? Why?

Get curious. Ask good probing questions (avoiding ones that give you only yes or no answers), and you'll gain a deeper understanding of what really matters to your employees. Be patient with people who've never had a boss ask these kinds of questions and might be uncomfortable responding initially. Embrace reflective silence. Don't be afraid of it. Some managers ask how their employees would like to communicate about their career interests. Sometimes a questionnaire to help them prepare works well.

Step 2: Offer Your Perspective

Help your employees reflect on their own reputations, on the feedback they've gotten from others, and on the areas they need to develop. And give them honest feedback regularly.

Think back to the last performance review you gave. It probably was based on past performance and connected to that employee's raise. Development feedback is different. It is future oriented and focuses on areas where the employee can improve.

Employees want specific feedback with examples of their performance and the effect on their future goals. Have them seek out colleagues at all levels who will give them a more realistic self-portrait to help them develop faster and smarter. And remember—development feedback includes good news as well as corrective input.

→ TRY THIS

Include these questions in your conversation:

★ What is the most helpful feedback you have received? How did it change your behavior? How did you apply that to your work?

★ In which areas do you wish I would give you more feedback? How can I help you feel more accomplished and successful at work?

★ Which of your team skills are most valued by your colleagues? How do you know? Whom might you ask? Based on their feedback, which skills do you hope to improve?

Think about all the awkward conversations you've had with employees whose career goals are simply out of sync with reality given their strengths and weaknesses. Our hunch is that the absence of honest feedback kept them out of sync. Employees continually tell us that they want straight talk. Want to keep them? Level with them.

Step 3: Discuss Trends

Help your employees consider their options by encouraging them to look beyond your department to detect shifts and changes that might impact their careers. Think about your company's growth areas and limitations as well as emerging skills the industry will require. Share this information with your employees. Helping your employees see what's down the road is a sign of respect, even if it isn't all good news.

ALAS

Lenore was exactly what our organization needed. She was young and wanted to use her technical as well as managerial skills, wanted to develop business, and in fact had already brought some in. She decided to look for a new job when she heard that there were some changes coming in our organization, and she realized she didn't know what would happen to her. She said that her first manager was great at coaching and keeping her in the loop but that she had recently been moved to work for another manager who had shown no interest in her career. So with the threat of impending change, and a manager who didn't seem to care, she took an offer at a small start-up company. She was clear that it was not the salary and benefits that drew her. It was the hope of a better manager, one who would keep her in the loop and care about her career. The exit interview lasted 90 minutes. I asked her if she would reconsider. She declined.

—Human resources manager

Clearly, a good career conversation with her new manager could have influenced Lenore's decision to look for other opportunities.

→ TRY THIS

Find out what your employees know about the trends in these areas:

★ Major economic, political, technological, and social changes taking place that will have the greatest effect on your organization

★ Opportunities and problems ahead

★ The biggest changes in your industry

★ How their profession will be different in the next two to five years

★ What really counts for success in your organization

★ Which websites, trade publications, journals, and organization newsletters provide information on industry and business trends

★ What new opportunities are available (e.g., international assignments, new businesses opening within the organization)

You don't have to take this all on your own shoulders. For example, you could have each person on your team research one of these areas and bring the information to the next staff meeting for discussion. But you do have to ensure that your employees know what's going on in your organization. By suggesting others who can provide additional perspectives on these and other issues, you open channels for your employees and give them a closer look at the key business needs of the organization. Have you done this lately?

Managers who talk openly and honestly about the future with their teams help employees envision the future and prepare for success. Constant change makes this strategy a critical piece in building a resilient team—a team that will be ready to meet the challenges ahead.

Step 4: Discover Multiple Options

Help your employees consider multiple career goals while they grow within their current positions. When employees analyze their potential development goals in terms of business needs and the strategic intent of the organization, everyone wins.

Caution! The employee is still primarily responsible for his or her career. Our suggestions do not mean *telling* the person what to do. Instead, offer choices for employees to analyze and consider.

Offering choices is important but sometimes difficult. For generations, the only acceptable career direction has been up. Actually, that is still often true in many cultures and companies. But *up is not the only way!*[1] There are at least four other ways employees can move their careers along. See the Goals chapter for more information.

→ TRY THIS

Help your employees answer these challenging questions:

★ Do you have enough information about the organization's current activities and plans to select several career goals?

★ How can you get the information you need?

★ Have you considered all available directions in selecting your career options?

★ Do your options adequately cover a variety of scenarios?

★ Should you select more career options?

★ Are your goals compatible with organizational goals and plans?

Once you have helped your employees look at options so that not all their plans reflect the vertical mindset, they will feel as if they have more leverage to manage their own careers.

Step 5: Codesign an Action Plan

Collaborate with your talented employees to design action steps that will increase their commitment to a career plan. Consider all the steps the employees would have to take to realize their best career goals, and develop contingency plans for each. Later, if one path is blocked, you already will have laid out other paths together.

Help your employees identify the obstacles they could encounter in following each path, and brainstorm ways around the obstacles. During the process, help them remember and maximize the assets they already have.

Leaders will have to learn what the successful conductors of the symphony orchestra have long known: The key to greatness is to look for people's potential and spend time developing it.[2]

→ TRY THIS

Ask any or all of these questions. The answers form the action plan.

★ What skills would you need to gain to help you achieve your goals?

★ What abilities do you already have that would help you toward any of your goals?

★ Who is in your network already who might open a door for you?

★ What training could I make available to fill the gaps you see?

★ What kinds of on-the-job development could help you move closer to several of your options?

Remember, your job is to help your employees identify the skills, development opportunities, and knowledge areas required for each alternative. Your job is not to build their plans but to support them.

If You Manage Managers

After you've held the next career discussion with a manager on your team, ask her how the career chats with *her* people are going. What is she learning about what people want next? How can she help "job sculpt" and develop the talent on her team? Step up the action: include career management goals in performance objectives for next year.

BOTTOM LINE

Employees have one thing in common: they want to know that someone cares about their careers. And that someone should be you if you want engaged, productive people on your team. Help them find opportunities to shape their careers according to their own unique wants and needs. When you do this, you'll find your best employees will want to stay a while and build their careers in *your* organization.

CHAPTER FOUR

Dignity
SHOW RESPECT

Ponder this: How will they know you truly respect them?

The one behavior that talented people seldom tolerate for long is disrespect. In fact, in a survey of 20,000 employees worldwide, respondents ranked respect as the most important leadership behavior. And they reported more disrespectful and uncivil behavior each year.[1]

Another global study measured the gap between employers' and employees' perspectives about dignity at work. Four in five employers (81 percent) believe their employees are treated with dignity and respect regardless of their job, role, or level, compared with 65 percent of employees who feel the same. And nearly two-thirds of employers (65 percent) believe they make it possible for employees to have a healthy integration of work and personal life, compared with less than half (46 percent) of employees who agree.[2]

How are you doing in the dignity department? What would your employees say?

If you wish to engage and retain your talent, you must recognize each person's unique qualities and then demonstrate your respect in consistent, undeniable ways.

ALAS

The team looked forward to the new manager's arrival with a lot of anticipation and hope. The current supervisor, who would report to this manager, spent hours walking the new manager through the details of what the team did, shared organizational inputs and did rounds of introductions.

Within a couple of months, the new manager started hiring people from his previous organization and formed a clique within the team. The new manager left the supervisor out of major decisions and overruled him in front of internal clients. The existing team members felt alienated as the new manager ignored their contributions. The new employees from the manager's previous organization, meanwhile, were confidants and became decision makers. No wonder over 75 percent of the original team moved out that year.

—Hemant Taneja, Tattva Consulting, New Delhi, India

Could that happen at your workplace? Have you, or has someone you know (even one of your direct reports), ever left for reasons like that? What else drives good people away, and what can a manager do about it?

Manage Your Sloppy Moods

Honoring others and treating them with dignity and respect may mean managing your moods. Have you ever worked for someone with roller-coaster moods? You know, one day he's up; the next he's *way* down. While it is human to have ups and downs, it is grown-up to manage those moods so that they do not hurt others. Some call moods that have run amok *sloppy moods*. They are simply uncontrolled. Whatever is felt comes spilling out and slops all over employees (or family). The results can be embarrassment, hurt, anger, humiliation, and loss of dignity.

→ TRY THIS

★ If you are guilty of sloppy moods, take notice and take control. Get away from others while you work through your difficulties. Take a time-out.

★ If you happen to slop on someone, apologize. To err is human, and most people appreciate an apology; it is a sign of respect.

★ If you have a serious problem managing your moods, consider seeking help from a professional or your organization's Employee Assistance Program.

Are They Invisible?

My previous boss never said hello to me. He would walk right past me in the hall as if I did not exist or was invisible. He did say hello to every vice president. My new boss treats me with respect. I feel like she values me as a person, even though her job level is above mine. I love working here.

—Software engineer

When employees talk about the disrespect that drove them out the door to a new job, they sometimes refer to this feeling of invisibility. You might be simply lost in thought when you pass your employees in the hall and fail to acknowledge them. But they will notice and may feel less than honored or respected.

Note: Different cultures show respect differently. Our Asian colleagues say that while respect is key, bosses may not be likely to smile or greet their employees in the hallway; it's just not part of the culture. They also say that the bosses who do smile and say hello are sure to win over their people!

Notice your employees. Pay attention as you walk down the halls and say hello to them by name. Smile, shake hands, greet your employees, and introduce them to others, even those of higher rank. They will feel respected and definitely not invisible.

Trust Me

Is it hard for you to trust your team? Andy Grove, former chairman of Intel, wrote a book called *Only the Paranoid Survive*. Great title, but in practice it is a tough way to live!

What we know is that when you trust your employees, most will be trustworthy. They will feel honored and respected when you trust them with important tasks and heavy responsibilities and when you let them do things their way. When you fail to trust them, they will often feel dishonored, disrespected, and undervalued. And you can bet they will leave when a better opportunity presents itself.

If you doubt this, think about a time in your career when you had a boss who trusted you implicitly, trusted you to excel, trusted you with information or assets. How did you feel? How committed did you feel to the boss or the organization as a result?

ALAS

He simply could not learn to trust us. It was as if he thought we were all out to get him, and in the end it was almost a self-fulfilling prophecy. We knew we were worthy of his trust, and yet we almost began to feel guilty as he micromanaged us and constantly looked over our shoulders. We had to account for every minute of our time and every nickel we spent. Finally, it was just too demeaning. The entire team decided to find other employment and a boss who trusted us.

—Director, engineering firm

→ TRY THIS

★ Check out your own ability to trust others. Do you tend to offer trust as a gift or demand evidence of trustworthiness before you give it?

★ Try trusting your employees. Say you trust them, act like you trust them, and *really* trust them. Give them responsibility and then let them carry it out.

What's Fair Is Fair

Talented workers will leave a boss who is perceived to be unfair. Unfair treatment translates to disrespect in many employees' minds. Check out your communication approach and your actions with your employees. How do they view the decisions and changes that you make? What seems fair or unfair to them? Do you honor their ideas, and do you care about their reactions? If you don't, you will lose them.

Always do what is right. It will gratify most of the people, and astound the rest.

—Mark Twain

Anybody Home?

Sometimes busy bosses seem almost unreachable. Unless the sky is falling (by their definition), it is virtually impossible to get their attention. How do you respond when your employees need to reach you? An employee wants to leave early on Friday for his son's soccer match and asks you on the Monday before. Another employee needs your okay to attend a conference in two months. A third employee's wife has been hospitalized with a life-threatening illness. What do you do? Ideally, you respond quickly in all three cases.

Unfortunately, too many busy bosses tell the first and second employees that they will get back to them but never do. The employees feel unimportant and disrespected and have to either nag for an answer or forget the whole thing (but they never really do). And what do busy bosses do about the third employee? Too often: nothing. Treating an employee with dignity means acknowledging how difficult and unique this life situation is.

My mother was dying of cancer and lived 1,000 miles away. I was a wreck at work, unable to concentrate, and feeling so guilty about not being with her. My boss took me into his office and told me to take as much time as I needed to go and be with my mother in her final days. I will never forget that act. I felt so valued and respected by him that my commitment to the organization soared.
—Executive assistant, consulting firm

→ TRY THIS

★ Listen to your employees' wants and needs. Even concerns that seem small or insignificant are clearly important to them. Paraphrase their requests to ensure you heard them correctly.

★ Respond to their requests quickly. Don't wait for them to nag you.

★ Be aware and take steps to help employees in their times of need. They will pay you back a thousandfold.

Respect—in Any Language

You cannot respect and honor others unless you respect—even celebrate—the differences between people. Can you imagine how ineffective (and boring) your team would be if everyone thought, looked, and believed the same and had the same talents? Most of us readily accept the notion that diversity of talent and perspective strengthens a work group and contributes to excellent results.

Scott Page, author of *The Diversity Bonus: How Great Teams Pay Off in the Knowledge Economy*, describes two types of diversity: cognitive and identity. Identity diversity refers to differences in race, gender, sexual orientation, ethnicity, physical capabilities, and culture. A person's cognitive diversity encompasses his or her learning, experience, and problem-solving tools. You get a diversity bonus when you have a team of people who bring different cognitive tools and ways of thinking to a problem. When working on a tough problem, you'll want smart people who think in a variety of ways, not just smart people.[3]

So, we can agree that diversity in the workplace often yields great results. Yet if we are honest, we admit that differences also get in the way. The hard truth is that many of us more often tolerate than celebrate differences.

> *Here is how the Museum of Tolerance in Los Angeles welcomes its visitors. As tour groups form in the lobby, they are invited into a waiting room that admits them into the museum. Our tour guide said to us, "Notice that there are two doors through which you may enter this museum. One is marked 'prejudiced' and the other is marked 'unprejudiced.' You may enter through whichever door represents you."*
>
> *In my tour group, there was a long pause as people pondered which door to choose. Finally, a man bravely stepped forward and turned the knob on the door marked "unprejudiced." A few stepped forward to follow him, while the rest of us watched. He turned the knob, looked a little confused, and then turned red with embarrassment as he realized the door was locked. We could only enter the museum through the door marked "prejudiced."*
>
> —Sharon Jordan-Evans

Which door would you have chosen? We all need to self-reflect, to take a good look at our preferences, prejudices, unconscious biases, inclinations, and leanings. We all have them. They pop up when we mentor and coach, promote, reward, punish, and hire (research shows we are most apt to hire someone like ourselves). Once you take note of your biases, you can begin to see the impact they might have on your employees.

The issue is how we respond. The first step in leveraging differences is to take a good look at your own beliefs. How much do you respect people who are very different from you? Do you value what they bring to your team? Does your entire team value what others bring to the conversation? How sincerely do you want them to stay?

Diversity is being invited to the party; inclusion is being asked to dance.

—Vernā Myers

Analyze Your Inclinations

The following list might help you recognize an unconscious bias. While it is long, it is no doubt incomplete. One reader said, "I see several listed biases I might be guilty of, but there is definitely one missing here. I shy away from people who don't like dogs!" We added her bias to the list.

Thanks to diversity specialist Pat Pope for helping us greatly expand our list.[4]

Appearance	Management status	Hobbies
Nationality	Work style	Sexual orientation
Language	Religion	Political affiliation
Education	Work habits	Socioeconomic
Height or weight	Marital status	background
Work content	Union affiliation	Military experience
Title	Job function or level	Mental abilities
Accent	Personal status	Income
Division, department,	Age	Race
group	Lifestyle	Ethnicity
Geographic origin	Parental status	Thinking style
Learning style	Gender	Physical abilities
Seniority	Talent	Pet affinity
Personality		

Now that you've read the list, consider the following:

★ There might be other things you'd add to the list. What do you tend to lean toward or away from?

★ Notice how your *biases* play out at work. Whom did you last promote? Whom do you tend to ignore, praise less often, and be less friendly with? Whom do you really *listen* to most often?

★ Learn about the differences among your employees. To accomplish this, one manager held a discovery day, where people were encouraged to talk about themselves, how they grew up, the holidays they observe, and why. Imagine how much you would learn about why your employees behave as they do and how much deeper your understanding would be.

★ Leverage the differences. The late Roosevelt Thomas, a diversity consultant and author, believed that diversity is "the maximum utilization of talent in the workforce."[5] Appreciate and use the individual strengths, styles, and talents of the people on your team. Are you doing that?

★ *Decide* to change. Practice inclusion and fairness. Consciously avoid discriminating in the old familiar ways. Your employees will notice.

Remember that there is no genetic predisposition to bias; no bias gene rides on your chromosomes; no DNA test can identify who is biased and who is not. Bias is learned. It's an acquired habit of thought rooted in fear and fueled by conditioning and, as such, can be unacquired and deconditioned. That's good news because no one can afford to allow his or her distorted vision to interfere with the ability to function effectively, fairly, and successfully in increasingly diverse workplaces.

—Sondra Thiederman

If You Manage Managers

Showing respect can be one of the toughest challenges for managers of managers. After all, showing respect, valuing diversity on the team, monitoring moods—all of this may seem difficult to measure and tricky to manage. Yet, it's part of your job. Your direct reports and those who report to them are watching how you deal with the disrespectful manager who reports to you. They want you to exercise courage, to mentor, to require behavior change, and sometimes even to *move* a disrespectful manager out of the role.

D

BOTTOM LINE

Attitudes are at the core of showing respect and honoring others. But actions are involved too. Actions that contradict verbal assurances of respect *erode* dignity. Check out your beliefs about differences and audit your actions. Listen to your employees, respond to them, and— bottom line—treat them with respect and dignity.

When you feel a sense of judgment,
ask yourself, "What do I not yet understand?"
—Pamela Weiss, Buddhist scholar

CHAPTER FIVE

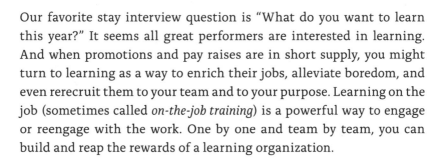

Enrich
ENERGIZE THE JOB

Ponder this: How often do your people have to leave to learn something new?

Our favorite stay interview question is "What do you want to learn this year?" It seems all great performers are interested in learning. And when promotions and pay raises are in short supply, you might turn to learning as a way to enrich their jobs, alleviate boredom, and even rerecruit them to your team and to your purpose. Learning on the job (sometimes called *on-the-job training*) is a powerful way to engage or reengage with the work. One by one and team by team, you can build and reap the rewards of a learning organization.

It Can Happen to Anyone
Did your own "job EKG" ever go flat? Did the feeling of challenge change to a feeling of routine? Did you think something was missing? What happened to your energy? In any case, did you start to wonder what else there was? Did you start to look around?

Unfortunately, your most valued employees are the most likely to suffer this sense of job discontent. By definition, they are savvy, creative, self-propelled, and energetic. They need stimulating work, opportunities for personal challenge and growth, and a contributing stake in the organizational action.

If good workers find that your company no longer provides these necessities, they may decide they have outgrown the place and will consider leaving or, worse yet, disengage on the job. If they disengage, their departure is psychological rather than physical. It shows up in absenteeism and mediocre performance. These people simply with-hold their energy and effort, figuring, "What's the point, anyway?"

Either way, through departure or disengagement, you lose talented people who are vital to the success of your unit and your company—a preventable loss.

ALAS

I had been doing the same work for seven years when my organiza-tion decided to expand the business in a new direction. I met with my boss to tell him that I would love to learn about the new side of the business and maybe expand my job to include at least some work in the new arena. I wasn't sure how it could all fit, but I knew I wanted something new and exciting in my day-to-day work life. When I raised the topic, he responded curtly, "The team has already been chosen to do this new work. We need you to keep doing what you're doing." That was the end of our discussion. I left the organi-zation six months later.

—Claims adjuster, insurance company

Get Enriched Quick

Job enrichment means a change in what your employees do (content) or how they do it (process), and it inevitably involves learning. Enrich-ment helps employees find the growth, challenge, and renewal they seek without leaving their current jobs, employers, or sometimes even their workstations.

An enriched job has one or more of these features:

★ Gives employees room to initiate, create, and implement new ideas

★ Promotes setting and achieving personal and group goals

★ Allows employees to see their contributions to an end product or goal

★ Challenges employees to expand their knowledge and capabilities (e.g., use technology to increase efficiency, productivity, or fun)

★ Allows employees to "job sculpt" and make the job they have a job they love

A job can be as neatly tailored to a worker's peculiar goals and requirements as a pair of Levi's [jeans] to an online customer's imperfect physique.

—David Ulrich and David Sturm

If enrichment is so beneficial, why isn't it a standard part of every job? One good reason is this: what enriches one employee is different from what enriches the next. Courtney, devastated by her job's predictability, craves variety in each day's tasks. Marcos, tired of being told how to do his audit reports, is ready to teach someone else how to do them. Sofia sees that her computer programs meet the needs of her superiors and now wants to spend more time creating useful applications for her colleagues.

How do you tailor job enrichment to individuals and their needs? Ask them what would enrich their jobs! You'll find their diverse answers are as unique as they are.

→ TRY THIS

Use these questions to help people probe for possibilities of enrichment. As you listen, help them find answers and options that would work for them.

★ In what ways is your job important to the company?

★ What skills do you use on the job? What talents and interests do you have that you don't use?

★ What about your job do you find challenging or rewarding? What's not challenging or rewarding?

★ How might you delegate more effectively and more often?

★ In what areas would you like increased responsibility?

★ What would you like to be doing in the next three to five years?

★ In what ways would you like your job to change?

★ What would you like to learn about different departments, cultural or ethnic groups, or senior leaders? How might we help you find a way to explore that?

Add to the list, and then ask these questions to help people evaluate their jobs and discover ideas for enrichment. Their responses will, and should, vary greatly from person to person.

The Learning Assignment

We said that learning is core to enrichment. Now let's look at how a learning assignment brought back the "juice" of the job for one employee and made his job EKG spike.

When Sergey's boss asked what he wanted to learn next year, he said, "I'd like to improve my negotiating skills." The boss said, "Great, let's do it," and they began a three-step learning process. Here are the steps they followed and how it worked out for Sergey:

> *Step 1. Conscious Observation. Sergey's boss selected an expert for Sergey to observe—someone who was exceptionally skilled at negotiating. After the observation, Sergey and his boss discussed what Sergey noticed, learned, and would mirror or do differently.*

> *Step 2. Selected Participation. Sergey's boss gave him the chance to take a well-defined but limited role in a negotiation (preparing the opening remarks with a vendor). The goal was to give Sergey an opportunity to get his feet wet without feeling overwhelmed. Following the meeting, Sergey and his boss discussed what worked and where there might be room for improvement.*

> *Step 3. Key Responsibility. Sergey's boss gave him primary responsibility for a project that required excellent negotiation skills. Sergey completed the entire negotiation with the vendor and was both visible and accountable for the outcome. His boss was present, of course, but would have stepped in only if Sergey requested his support.*

It worked. One year later, Sergey is thrilled with his job and continues to develop mastery as a negotiator for his organization.

Note: Any one of these steps can be the learning assignment, in and of itself.

Consider the Possibilities

The bedrock of most enrichment activities is learning. Yet enrichment can take many different forms. Remember to ask your talented employees what they'd like to do and how they'd like to do it.

In some cultures, employees expect their boss to manage their careers. They might have never engaged in enrichment activities or been so bold as to request them. Here are some techniques that work if you are careful to match them to individual wants and needs:

Form teams. Self-directed work groups can make a lot of their own decisions. They can redistribute work so that team members learn more, have more variety, and follow more projects through to completion.

Touch the client. A computer systems troubleshooter might be more effective knowing the needs of real people and units rather than responding only to problems as they occur. Assign one troubleshooter to one department (the client), and make him or her accountable for that client's success in using the company's computer system.

Rotate assignments. New responsibilities can help an employee feel challenged and valued. Employees can acquire important new skills that add depth to the workforce.

Increase feedback. Do more than annual reviews. Find ways to develop peer review and client review opportunities. Employees want to know about their performance, and continual feedback allows them to be their own quality control agents.

Involve employees in decisions. Employees are empowered and motivated when they take part in decisions that have an impact on their work, such as budget and hiring decisions, or ways to organize work and schedules. Involvement allows employees to see the big picture and enables them to make a contribution they find meaningful.

Practice delegating. Which tasks and projects have to be done by you? Which might you delegate to others? Not only will delegating more effectively get the work done, but you'll have more time for self-development, strategic decision-making, and action.

Nurture creativity. Untapped creativity dwindles. If employees rarely think for themselves, they lose the ability to contribute their best ideas. You can help by asking for and rewarding creative ideas, by giving employees the freedom and resources to create, and by challenging employees with new assignments, tasks, and learning.

Teach someone. Teaching another person is motivational for many. If an employee has a particular niche or specialty and enjoys passing this knowledge on, you have a perfect win-win!

Support enrollment in learning opportunities. German law provides for a *Bildungsurlaub,* five days off per year to participate in an approved training course. Although not many countries have a law like this, the idea of enriching a job via a learning experience is something any manager in any organization can explore.

Commit to an enrichment workout. Your employees' efforts don't have to take a lot of time but can lead to careers that are in much better shape than before. Discuss the following warm-up questions in your next career conversations.[1] Think calisthenics (table 5.1).

Table 5.1. Enrichment workout

	Reach up	What is something managers do that you've always wanted to take on?
	Reach out	What is something a colleague is currently doing that you would like to learn?
	Reach down	What are you willing to delegate that not only would give you some space but also would open up a learning opportunity for one of you colleagues
	Reach to the side	What ability do you have—something that comes easily to you—that you could teach, train, or mentor others in the group to do?

Give these job enrichment ideas to your employees. Ask them to add to the list and to get specific about the enrichment goals they're considering. Then have them choose two or three favorites.

What's in It for Me? My Team? My Organization?

Before employees lock on to their goals for the coming weeks or months, make sure they complete the Payoff Potential Quiz. Discuss the questions with them. Their answers to the quiz will help them decide which goals to pursue next.

Payoff Potential Quiz

If you choose this enrichment goal . . .

★ What's in it for you?

- How will it build your skills?
- How will it increase your marketability in your organization? In your profession?
- How will it enhance your reputation as a specialist or generalist?
- How will it help you gain more confidence and competence in your current position?
- How will it extend your network?
- How will it spice up your day-to-day work life?

★ What's in it for your work group?

- How will it help you work more effectively with your current team?
- How will it increase/enhance your contribution to your work group or department?
- How will it make your group members' lives better, easier, or more fun?

★ What's in it for the organization?

- How will it increase your value to the organization?
- How does it contribute to the current organizational mission, strategy, or goals?
- How does it address a current relevant business need?

Note: The "What's in it for you?" section is first and longest. That's on purpose!

As you think about job enrichment, don't feel as if you have to have all the answers, and don't let yourself become the "fix-it" person. Truly listen to your people. This is a collaborative process. Ultimately, your employees need to move the needle on their own job satisfaction—with your support, of course! We wrote a book to help them do just that. It's called *Love It, Don't Leave It: 26 Ways to Get What You Want at Work*.

If You Manage Managers

Enrichment activities are some of the least expensive, most effective of all engagement and retention strategies. Chat about enrichment possibilities with the managers you manage. Help them prepare for the conversations they'll have with their employees. Devote part of a staff meeting for managers to share creative enrichment activities they and their employees are planning.

BOTTOM LINE

If you help employees enrich their jobs, you can benefit them, their teams, and the entire organization. Stay alert to enrichment opportunities for all your employees. Encourage them to suggest ways to enrich their own jobs. Watch their job EKGs spike!

CHAPTER SIX

Family

GET FRIENDLY

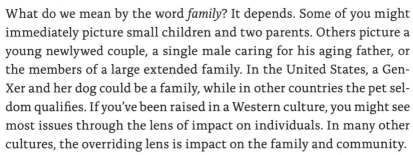

Ponder this: How often do your employees have to choose between work and family?

What do we mean by the word *family*? It depends. Some of you might immediately picture small children and two parents. Others picture a young newlywed couple, a single male caring for his aging father, or the members of a large extended family. In the United States, a Gen-Xer and her dog could be a family, while in other countries the pet seldom qualifies. If you've been raised in a Western culture, you might see most issues through the lens of impact on individuals. In many other cultures, the overriding lens is impact on the family and community.

Inclusive workplaces recognize that one family-friendly strategy won't meet all their employees' individual needs. It's critical to consider the different types of families in your group and then think about (and talk about) the approaches that will work best for each of them. Remember, the most accurate way to get this information quickly is simply to ask your employees.

People disengage or quit when rigid workplace rules cause unbearable family stress. Would they leave your organization over work/family conflicts? Yes. Business magazines have spent plenty of ink in recent years on the importance of developing a "family-friendly culture." But what does that term really mean?

Employees are asking for a workplace that helps them balance the demands of their work and family lives, rather than forcing them to choose one over the other. Today and from now on, organizations that are not family-friendly will definitely have a harder time finding and keeping good people.

Talented employees do not have to look far to find family-friendly employers who offer features like these:

★ Childcare facilities or subsidies

★ Flexible work schedules and locations

★ Job sharing

★ Eldercare assistance (such as referral programs)

★ Creative maternity or paternity leave programs (with no punishment for taking that leave)

★ Pet accommodations

Savvy employers give talented employees flexibility in how they work, when they work, and often where they work. They allow employees to meet personal responsibilities while still being productive at work.

If your organization does have these policies and perks in place, that's great. But if not, you have two options. One is to benchmark. Get smart about what other organizations are offering, and then go to your manager (or the human resources department) with information and suggestions. See if you can get some of these ideas adopted in your organization.

Whether or not you take the first option, you can take the more urgent one: become a more family-friendly manager. Start by modeling the behaviors you hope to see. One CEO told his staff that he wouldn't start meetings before nine o'clock because he takes a daily walk with his wife. He sent a loud message to his management team that it is acceptable, even desirable, to balance family with business goals.

There are many things that you can do to support your employees' lives outside work. The result will be more productive workers who are less likely to stray.

→ **TRY THIS**

Ask your employees questions like this: "What would make your life easier?" In their answers, look for small things that you, their manager, might be able to do to help. Brainstorm with your employees to create some innovative solutions to their work/family challenges. By the way, we believe that most people are basically decent and are not looking for ways to abuse your policies. They will value your trusting them and your efforts to make life easier.

Be Flexible

You may feel restricted by your organization's lack of family-friendly programs or policies. Yet you have tremendous opportunities to get family-friendly within your own work group. What you do as a manager can mean so much to your employees as they juggle work and family. And much of what you can do as a manager costs you and your organization little or nothing.

F

ALAS

Ernie was frustrated and exhausted trying to manage his work and family life. His wife also worked, and they had a six-month-old baby. Ernie wanted to partner with his wife in raising their child, so he began to flex his hours a bit to pick up the baby at childcare or take her to the doctor. His productivity and work quality remained high, but his hours dropped (from 55 to 45 a week) and looked somewhat erratic. The boss told Ernie that he simply had to return to his previous schedule—end of discussion. Even though Ernie tried to explain his needs, the boss had no time and no tolerance. Within two months Ernie had found a new job, one with a family-friendly culture and a boss who allowed him flexibility in his schedule.

Ernie's boss lost a valuable employee, one who may be very costly to replace, because he did not take the time to listen and to design a family-friendly work solution with his employee. Rigidity cost him dearly.

Think flexibly the next time an employee asks you for different work hours or time off to help a spouse, parent, or friend. Think about the real costs of saying yes. Will productivity suffer? Will you set a dangerous precedent? Will that employee begin to take advantage of you?

It is more likely that your employees will applaud (maybe silently) your open-mindedness and willingness to help a valued employee in a time of need. Remember to set clear expectations for your employees' results and hold them to those results. Then you will have room to flex when it matters. And that flexing will pay off!

Be Supportive

Some managers mistakenly think that they should clearly separate themselves from their employees' personal lives. You have much more to gain by showing your interest in their lives outside work.

> *I was so excited about my daughter's singing debut at her high school. She had been taking vocal lessons; she had developed a strong, beautiful voice; and that day was her chance to show it off. She would sing the national anthem (without accompaniment) during the all-school pep rally at one o'clock. My boss was excited for me and said, "No problem," when I asked him if I could go watch her. But here's the best part. When I returned, he asked me how it went and asked if I would show him the video. It was such a small thing but meant so much to me.*
>
> —Receptionist, manufacturing firm

We have heard about managers who became involved in several appropriate ways. As you read these approaches, think about which ones might work for you and your employees:

★ Allowing employees' children to come to work with them occasionally, usually to celebrate a special occasion or because of a special need

★ Driving to an employee's house to offer support and condolences following a death in the family

★ Accompanying employees to their children's ball games and recitals

★ Inviting an employee and his or her parents, relatives, or children to lunch

★ Allowing well-behaved pets into the workplace

★ Staying late after work to help employees work on Halloween costumes for their children

★ Researching eldercare alternatives for an employee who needs help with aging parents

★ Sending birthday cards or cakes to employees' family members

★ Setting up special email and resource areas on the company intranet for employees' children

★ Locating resources (the company lawyer) for an employee struggling with the health insurance company

Here is an example of really showing support:

When people ask me why I stayed at my company for 27 years, I tell them this story: When I was pregnant with my first child— he's now 24—I had trouble with my pregnancy and was sent home for bed rest. After two weeks, I couldn't take it anymore and went back to work, commuting daily by subway. The president of the company called me and said, "We so value what you bring to this organization. We want to help as you rejoin the team." For two months, he arranged a ride for me to and from work every day. At that time, I became a lifetime employee of that organization.

—Chair and CEO, advertising agency

Be Creative

"We've never done that here." "The policies don't support that." "I'd be in trouble with my boss if I allowed that." "If I did this for you, I'd have to do it for everyone." These are common excuses among managers who don't know their real power or are afraid to test the limits of the family-friendly (or -unfriendly) rules. Sure, there are constraints and policy guidelines in most organizations. And you have to play by those rules to some degree. But often it pays to get creative on behalf of your employees and their needs. Job sharing is just one example of a creative solution to a challenging situation.

There was no such thing as job sharing in this organization. We have a long history and cemented policies. After the birth of our children, another director and I decided to go to our boss and ask about the possibility of sharing one job. The job was high level and critical to the organization, so at first there was tremendous concern about even trying it. But our boss took a risk and gained approval for a six-month test period. That was 12 years ago, and we have been sharing the job effectively ever since. Our boss's creativity and flexibility allowed us both to balance family and work. We are tremendously grateful and loyal employees.

—Manager, public utility

★ If employees must travel on weekends, offer something in exchange, such as time off during the week or allowing family members to travel with the employee.

★ When your employees travel to areas where they have family or friends, allow them to spend extra time with those people at the beginning or end of the trip.

★ If company policy absolutely prohibits bringing pets to work, consider a picnic in a park where those furry family members are welcome.

★ Give your employees a "floating" day off each year to be used for a special occasion. Or suggest they go home early on their birthdays or anniversaries.

★ Have a party for your team and their families. Invite the kids (or hire sitters for small ones), and go for pizza together.

★ When an employee asks about working from home, really explore that possibility. What are the upsides? Downsides? Get creative about how that might work to benefit both the employee and your team.

★ Consider subsidizing your employees' home internet service costs. The monthly costs for internet use are small compared with the productivity you'll get in return. This also allows them to work effectively from home.

The best kind of creativity is collaborative. Remember to brainstorm a list of ideas *with your employees* and be continuously open to new and innovative ways to balance family and work. Tailor and customize your strategies to employees' needs.

Balance by Any Other Name

As the times change, so does the language. Right now, as you read this book, managers might be talking about work-life integration or blending versus balancing or something else altogether. No matter how you name it, it's still about finding a way for your treasured, talented people to have both—a great job and a wonderful family life.

If You Manage Managers

What if you're a family-friendly manager, but a manager you manage is not? You can help him change. Be a strong role model. Walk your talk. Your people watch how you prioritize and choose between work and home events, and they might just follow in your footsteps. Coach them to flex, to partner creatively with employees as they struggle to balance work and life. If you set the stage, show it can be done, and reward family-friendly managers, you'll create a team that's a magnet for talent.

F

BOTTOM LINE

Flexible work arrangements and the core belief that work is something you "do," not "somewhere you have to be," is a winning engagement strategy. Do some of the ideas in this chapter seem beyond what you could implement in your workplace? If your definition of *family-friendly* is allowing your employees to accept a personal phone call, it's time to learn what's going on around you. There are positive payoffs for your efforts, including increased loyalty, money saved, and the competitive edge that a loyal and productive workforce will provide. Become a family-friendly manager, and keep your talent on your team.

CHAPTER SEVEN

Goals

EXPAND OPTIONS

Ponder this: How many career paths do they see?

You're inundated with goals. You have performance goals for yourself—and for your employees. You (and they) also have life goals, financial goals, athletic goals, spiritual goals, balance goals, maybe even weight-loss goals!

Here, we'll be focusing on career-related goals. You've no doubt set goals for your learning, your growth, and your success at work. Have you linked arm in arm with your treasured, talented people to set these kinds of goals?

Remember to include *everyone* in the adventure: differently abled, younger or older, people of color, differently gendered, frontline to senior-level workers. Keep an open mind as you discuss options to help them excel and, in the process, increase the odds they'll stay with you for a while.

You Want to Move Where?

Do you get a knot in your stomach when a valued employee begins a conversation with one of these phrases?

★ I'd like to talk to you about my career.

★ I really want to understand what my career options are.

★ I'm interested in talking about my next step.

★ I don't understand why she got that promotion. I thought I . . .

★ Only a step up makes me feel appreciated.

Feel the knot? It's understandable. You value employees with superb skills who have mastered the current job and want more. They may get calls from recruiters. They want a chance to run a project. They're in your office, looking to you for a much-needed, much-deserved conversation about moving up in the organization. You want to keep them. And "up" is in short supply.

You may lose some of them. However, our 25 years of research reveals that not all those who say they want vertical moves will leave if they don't get them. But they *will* leave (physically or psychologically) if they are not being challenged, growing, and having new experiences. So what can you do for them if up is not an option?

Moving Forward Instead of Up

What if your employees began to think about other ways of moving? What if each move challenged and rewarded them? What if they could move forward instead of up?

Sometimes you can prevent turnover by helping your employees identify several career goals. If employees see that you can support several viable alternatives, they will picture a future for themselves within your organization.

> *I was ready for a promotion, and it looked like there was no place for me at the next level. Then my manager told me about an opportunity to work in the Seattle operation. I jumped at the chance and have been here thirteen years now. Initially the adjustment was tough, but the challenges and growth have been unbelievable—probably even better than had I gotten my sought-after promotion in Dublin.*
>
> —Microsoft programmer from Dublin

Right Person, Right Place, Right Time

Human resource professionals and managers often repeat the phrase "Right person, right place, right time." It's never been easy to achieve. But here's a twist to consider: what if there were more *right* places? Would there not be more *right* times for all those *right* people?

We believe that inside any organization there are four possible moves in addition to moving up. We also believe that the more specifically you can outline those moves, the less likely your talented employees will see *other* grass as greener. Consider talking with your employees about moves in several directions.

Possible Career Options

Not everyone wants to move up. Yet it is common to assume people do. As you consider the following options, notice your biases toward or away from these choices. Can you discuss each of them with equal enthusiasm?[1]

★ Enrichment: Growing in place

★ Lateral movement: Moving across or horizontally

★ Exploration: Temporarily moving to research other options

★ Realignment: Moving downward to open new opportunities

If you notice that three of these options (all but enrichment) raise the possibility of your talented people moving away from you, you're right. If this makes you nervous, you're in the majority. If you've built a strong, functioning team, you don't want to lose key talent to other managers and other parts of the organization. Some managers are so fearful that they hoard their talent, failing to expose their team members to other opportunities. Ironically, that strategy backfires and some of the best people walk—often to the competitor.

So why should you help your best people expand their options, even if it means they leave your team? Here are some possibilities:

★ People love to work for someone who cares enough to help them with their careers. They'll actually stay a little longer with a development-minded manager.

★ You will gain a reputation as a manager who cares about people and their development. That reputation will draw other talented people your way.

★ You may gain personal satisfaction from helping others develop.

★ Your efforts could save talent for the enterprise. This is truly your job.

Enrichment

Enrichment is probably the most important option to discuss—but it's also one of the most ignored. Most folks seem to think they need to move out of their current position to develop. Never has this been less true. Most of your employees' work is changing constantly. Job enrichment means a change in what your employees do (content) or how they do it (process), and it inevitably involves learning.

The term *upskilling* is often used to describe company, industry, or community initiatives designed to expand people's capabilities and employability and thus fulfill the talent needs of a rapidly changing economy. Enrichment activities play a key role in upskilling efforts.

Here's the critical question for you (and them) to ponder: what can employees do, or learn to do, that will energize their work and bring them closer to achieving their goals and the goals of the organization?

> *I worked for a great boss as a project manager, but I knew (and she really knew too) that I could do more. I had fantastic artistic skills (if I do say so myself), and my boss did something about it. She sent me to graphic recording school and has used my new skills in her business. I am thrilled!*
>
> —Project manager

Be sure your employees understand that enrichment goals can prepare them for future moves and enhance or add to their skills.

→ TRY THIS

For clues about potential enrichment opportunities, ask your employees questions like these:

★ What do you enjoy most about your job?

★ What could be added to your job to make it more satisfying?

★ What assignment would advance you further in your current work?

★ Which of your current tasks is the most routine? Whom might you train to take this over?

★ What talent do you have that your manager may not be aware of and that you'd like to use more?

Building on the new information, develop a plan with your employees that would help them move toward a meaningful personal goal.

Lateral Movement

Until recently, lateral moves meant that your career might be headed for a dead end. Not today. Sideways moves no longer sideline talent. Instead, they often offer much-needed breadth of experience and can be key to achieving one's career goals.

Taking a lateral move should mean applying current experience in a new job at the same level but with different duties or challenges. Help employees see that lateral moves can improve skills or shift them from a slow-growing function to an expanding part of the organization.

G

→ TRY THIS

To trigger ideas about potential lateral moves, ask your employees questions like these:

★ Which of your skills can be applied beyond your present job and present department?

★ If you make a lateral move, what long-term career opportunities would it provide?

★ What three skills are most transferable to another department?

★ What other department interests you?

Once you're armed with answers to these questions you can begin to explore lateral move opportunities with your talented employees.

Exploration

It happens: we reach a stage in our careers when we aren't sure of what we want or what choices are available or even what's appropriate. We need information to decide if the grass is indeed greener elsewhere. Encourage your people to consider options like these:

★ Taking short-term job assignments in other parts of the organization or in other parts of the world

★ Participating on project teams with people from other departments

★ Scheduling informational interviews (interviews with people whose job your employee *thinks* he or she wants)

Giving a talented person whose expertise you need the chance to explore other teams isn't easy. But people are less likely to feel trapped in their current jobs when they have other choices. They may find out that the grass isn't greener.

→ TRY THIS

For exploration ideas, ask your employees the following questions:

★ What other areas of the company interest you?

★ If you could start your career over, what would you do differently?

★ Which of our current organization task forces interest you? Which might give you the best view of another part of this organization?

★ Whose job would you like to learn more about?

★ If you could choose any person to shadow for a day, who would it be and why?

Now, discuss the "so what" of their answers. Whom might they talk to next about these possibilities?

Realignment

In the old world of "up is the only way," moving downward would probably be last on anyone's list of options. Even today we sometimes notice a bias or a negative perception about such a move. But sometimes the path to a career goal involves a step back to gain a better position for the next move. Realignment can relieve job stress or allow a graceful return to a role as an individual contributor.

ALAS

An excellent technical contributor was promoted to manager. At first he liked the work. It still had some technical components, and he managed other bright individual contributors. In time though, he felt he had made a mistake and longed to return to a technical position.

> *He had outgrown his previous position but wanted something with the new hardware group. He went to his manager to admit his mistake and request a move. His manager resisted, suggesting he give it more time or that he enroll in a training course to improve his management skills. Instead, he applied for and got a job that was precisely what he wanted—with a competitor.*

This company lost a talented person because neither he nor his manager discussed realignment.

In contrast, here's an example of successful realignment:

G

> *I was promoted to nursing director in a long-term-care facility, and at first I was thrilled. Two years later I realized that the job was too big. I got home exhausted and late every night and missed tucking my young kids into bed. I couldn't seem to blend the work with my family life. I talked with my manager about returning to my previous nonmanagement role. She understood and said yes. I remain so grateful for her understanding and I truly love my job!*
>
> —Registered nurse

→ TRY THIS

When considering realignment as an option, ask questions like these:

★ If you take an assignment in another area, what will be the new opportunities for growth and development?

★ How could a realigned position enable you to use the skills you really enjoy?

★ Do you miss the technical, hands-on work you used to do?

★ How might we positively communicate this move to the organization?

The answers to these questions can provide a wake-up call for your talented employees. Help them think about the pluses and the minuses of making this move.

When Up Is the Only Way

Rarely does anyone move in a solely vertical trajectory throughout a career. Yet sometimes your talented employees determine that up is the only choice for them. Your job then is to identify and communicate potential vertical options. Of course, advancement is most likely when an employee's abilities match the needs of the organization. You'll do well to explain the organization's strategic direction to your team so that individuals select assignments that will prepare them for coming changes and openings.

Clearly, technical excellence and political savvy are both critical to gaining that next step. Talented people need straight feedback and continual coaching to reach their vertical career goals. As you hold these discussions, remind your employees of two key considerations:

★ Always use the current job to ready yourself for vertical moves.

★ Talk with others who are in the desired position to better understand all aspects of the job.

→ TRY THIS

When discussing possible promotions with your employees, ask them questions like these:

★ Who is your competition for that next position? What are the other person's strengths and weaknesses?

★ How has your job performance been during the last year? How has it prepared you for the next step?

★ What's in it for this company to move you up?

★ What are the satisfactions and headaches that might come with this vertical move?

The More Choices, the Better

After reading this chapter, one manager said, "This seems like a lot of asking. Shouldn't my employees come to me with their thoughts and requests about their careers?" Sure they should. But sometimes they won't. They'll be quiet; they'll wait for you to offer an interesting option—and they'll leave when it doesn't happen.

An Asian colleague said, "Employees are generally hesitant to speak out about their career plans because it is perceived as being overly ambitious and not loyal to the current boss." Similarly, in Latin America, employees are likely to *wait to be asked* to move into a new role.

Take cultural and individual differences into account. Avoid assumptions about what people want and how they hope to discuss those wants with you. Ask, then tailor your approach to every talented individual on your team.

If You Manage Managers

G

Sometimes the managers you manage are worried they can't give promotions to their well-deserving stars. And they worry that when they can't offer those coveted moves up the ladder, their talent will disengage or depart. Help them expand the list of options their own employees have for growth and fulfillment.

BOTTOM LINE

Helping employees reach their goals often means helping them consider moves they may not have seriously considered before. Ask the questions from this chapter to help them see what they could gain by trying a move that isn't a simple vertical step. The more options you can *create with them*, the more you will increase your organization's chances of keeping treasured talent.

Note: One reason talented people leave is because their manager hoarded them. You may have to let them go to let them grow. You might lose them from your team but save them for the enterprise!

CHAPTER EIGHT

Hire

FIT IS IT

Ponder this: What was your best hire ever?
How can you repeat that?

You've heard the adage "Start with the end in mind," right? The perfect ending is that the people you work so hard to recruit (from inside or outside the organization) turn out to be exactly right for the jobs you hire them to do! They love being on your team and working for you. And they stay for a while.

The love 'em approach to engaging and retaining talent starts with the hiring process. Why? Because getting the right people in the door in the first place increases the odds of keeping them. As the manager, you have the clearest sense of the right fit for your department. Seems logical, doesn't it? Yet some managers see selection as a less important part of their jobs. They spend little time identifying the critical success factors for a position, preparing and conducting excellent interviews based on those factors, and, finally, evaluating and comparing the candidates before making a hiring decision. They may even delegate much of the hiring process to human resources instead of being involved themselves.

Hiring is, in fact, among the most important tasks you have as a manager, and you'll be doing a lot more of it, as baby boomers (the largest generation in the workforce) continue to leave the workplace and you search for their replacements. Globally, hiring remains a critical engagement and retention strategy. And it doesn't stop with the job offer. *Today rerecruiting your best people is as critical as hiring them in the first place.* More about that later.

What Is Right Fit?

How do you know if a candidate will fit? How do you measure fit, manage your biases, and make more objective hiring decisions? How do you leverage cognitive diversity to strengthen your team? Right fit does not mean "like me." It's tempting to hire people like yourself—in looks, personality, style, experience, and more. Be aware of that temptation as you embark on a hiring project.

Several years ago, one company embraced a diversity goal and changed its hiring criteria accordingly. *Fit* was defined according to what truly matters most going forward in the business, not looking backward. The team is much more diverse today, and the organization is more successful than ever in its history.

> *Berrett-Koehler's philosophy is to hire people who have demonstrated a track record of success in accomplishing significant advances in complex and challenging environments—in any areas, whether previous jobs or volunteer work or entrepreneurial projects, not necessarily in book publishing. BK's philosophy is also to seek employees who bring cultural, ethnic, social, and intellectual diversity to Berrett-Koehler rather than employees who are like current BK employees in appearance, background, knowledge, or interests. We seek employees who have shown that they perform well in environments that are participative, flexible, creative, high in individual initiative, and high in self-accountability.*
>
> —Berrett-Koehler, our publisher

Measuring Fit

When a person has skills, experience, and interests that match the job requirements, as well as core values that are consistent with the organization's values, you have the right fit. Remember to look deeply and widely inside your organization, just in case that right-fit person is already in your midst!

> *Southwest Airlines looks for fit, especially with the company culture. A pilot told us about his own interview and selection process. He had heard that Southwest managers "hire for attitude and*

train for skill." The interviews they conducted with him certainly seemed to support that rumor. Through multiple interviews, he realized that the interviewers seemed to care more about who he was as a person than the fact that he had a stellar aviation background that should have made him an obvious choice. They probed for attitudes, beliefs, and behaviors that would give them clues about how he might treat flight attendants or peers, how he might deal with conflict at work, and what mattered most to him. Southwest managers tested his sense of humor in many ways during the series of interviews, and it became clear to him that they were truly looking for a fit between the way work gets done at Southwest Airlines and his personality.

Why does Southwest care about an employee's sense of humor, especially a pilot's? Because Southwest's values include providing "outrageous customer service" and having *fun* at work.

Fit also means alignment between the job requirements and the candidate's skills, experience, and interests. How often have you seen employees leave (on their own or with a push) because they simply did not have the right skills or interests? Why didn't the hiring manager see the problem at the outset? How can you avoid that expensive mistake? Do your homework, be prepared, and be clear about your wants and needs.

What are the "must-haves" for the position? Consultants Connie Bentley and Linda Rogers shared part of a sample grid with us (table 8.1):

Table 8.1. Hiring criteria

THE CANDIDATE MUST	OR
Have experience in our industry	Demonstrate how other-industry experience can add value to our business
Live close enough to be in the office daily	Be willing to commute long distances to work
Have an MBA	Have other relevant postgraduate education
Leap tall buildings in a single bound	Leap smaller buildings but more of them

Are you smiling?

→ TRY THIS

★ First, find talent in your midst. Too often, the right fit is right in front of you and it's overlooked. You think you'll find the perfect person for this job from outside. But is that true? Look around; ask other leaders about amazing people who might qualify. Then include those frequently hidden gems in your job search process.

★ Analyze the job. Get input from others to clarify the tasks, traits, and style required. Then create interview questions that will help you decide if the person has these skills or traits.

★ Create an interview guide with carefully crafted behavioral questions. Behavioral questions allow you to learn how candidates have handled certain situations. Their answers will help you predict their ability to handle similar situations in the future. Use the same questions for all candidates so that you can make fair comparisons.

★ Include others in the interview process. Have potential team members and peers of these future employees interview them (ideally asking different questions from yours) and give you their input. Several heads are definitely better than one when it comes to hiring.

★ Consider using personality and skill assessments to help you make the decision. Get information from your human resources department about tools that might help you evaluate candidates' skills, work interests, and even values. Note: Don't rely on just one tool when making your decision.

In Search of Fit

Ramesh, a manager in a high-tech global firm, has an opening for a supervisor in the marketing department in Switzerland. He placed ads on job boards and in newspapapers and netted a stack of résumés to consider. With help from his human resources representative, he has narrowed the field to the top 10 candidates. On paper, all 10 have technical skills that are great fits for the job.

Ramesh has identified his department's core values (honesty, integrity, teamwork, and customer focus) and leadership competencies (motivating others, building a team, and dealing with ambiguity). He creates an interview guide with inquiries like these:

★ Tell me about a work incident when you were totally honest, despite a potential risk or downside for the honesty.

★ How did you handle a recent situation where the direction from above was unclear and circumstances were changing?

★ Describe how you motivated a group of people to do something they did not want to do.

Note that the questions are open-ended, so they can't be answered yes or no. They are behavioral, forcing the candidates to cite real-life examples. Ramesh probes to learn more, takes notes, and later compares his findings with other interviewers. While there is no such thing as a totally objective interview or selection process, this method allows Ramesh to make the most objective decision possible.

→ TRY THIS

★ Remember to sell your company to talented prospects honestly. Think about what makes your company unique and a great place to work.

★ Listen carefully to what candidates are seeking. Be open to possibilities. Example: One company enticed its top choice by changing the job title from Feed Salesman to Livestock Produce Specialist.

★ Place a copy of this book on your desk during the interview. (Candidates will get the hint that keeping good people is important to you.) To go a step further, show them the book and ask them which of the chapters (A–Z) are most relevant to retaining *them*.

What Do You Assume?

What if *right fit* means "like me" or "the right age, accent, shape/size, gender, or color?" It doesn't—or shouldn't. The right-fit excuse has been used many times to put clones (usually clones of the boss) in jobs. That is certainly not what we mean by *right fit*. In fact, if you spend the time to identify those critical factors that spell success for a particular job and then select people using those criteria, you are most apt to avoid dismissing potentially wonderful candidates.

We all have leanings (unconscious biases), and we often make assumptions based on them. Let's test some of your assumptions about getting the right person in the job. Ask yourself, as you read the following list, "Have I ever thought this about a person or a job?" Be brutally honest—you don't have to tell anyone how you responded!

Assumption Testing

The following are sample assumptions. What do *you* assume?

Assumption: Single mothers will be a risk because when their children are ill, they will not show up.

Fact: Some single moms so need this job that they will find a way to make it to work. Some have excellent contingency planning skills and have two or three backup plans when the kids are sick.

Assumption: He is too old or too young for this job.

Fact: What's age got to do with it? Architect Frank Lloyd Wright and heart surgeon Michael DeBakey are examples of people who excelled in their crafts after the age of 90.

Assumption: We need a man in this job because it is too challenging for a woman.

Fact: The ability to function well is made up of a combination of traits, skills, behaviors, and experience that is *gender-neutral* (meaning gender does not predict ability).

Assumption: Someone of _____ descent just wouldn't be comfortable or really fit in here.

Fact: If you've ever studied or worked in a multicultural environment, you know that a person's heritage has no bearing on his or her comfort or fit within a particular environment. Think about your own experiences and where you've fit in just fine, despite dramatic language or cultural differences.

When you find yourself forming assumptions about candidates based on their gender, size, accent, attire, or color (and, by the way, we all do that sometimes), then gently move yourself back to the key criteria you have identified and your methodology for assessing all your candidates fairly.

Avoid Desperation Hiring

Love 'em managers care enough to wait for the right fit. They care about the candidates' and the teams' ultimate success and satisfaction.

Our colleagues in Asia tell us that with economic growth comes a lot of pressure to "get warm bodies" into seats, particularly in China, Singapore, and India. When candidates are few and your needs are immediate, you, too, can fall victim to the dangerous syndrome of *desperation hiring*. When your only interview question is "When can you start?" or "Can you fog a mirror?" (as in, "Are you breathing?"), you know you're in trouble.

If you're tempted to resort to desperation hiring, remember that today's hiring mistake is tomorrow's headache. You know how hard it is to rid your team of the wrong hire. (Someone recently suggested we write a sequel to *Love 'Em* called *How to Lose Your Losers*. Her point is well taken!)

Prevent Quick Quits

Your risk of losing talent is highest in the first three to six months on the job. Why might that be? Too often we choose the right people but fail to support them as they assume their new roles. It is crucial that you extend the handshake in ways that matter to each new hire.

Orientation (also known as onboarding) *and ongoing support* are key pieces of the selection process and will increase the odds of your new hires' success, contribution to, and tenure on the team. New hires come to an organization fully charged, excited about their new adventure, and filled with energy and potential. By effectively tapping into that energy, knowledge, and wisdom right from the start, you can maximize new employees' potential and productivity well past the first year.

We know that many quick quits *can* be prevented. There is a direct correlation between shortened tenure and actions you do, or do not, take (yup, sorry—*you* again). Develop a relationship. Show you care. Start by having conversations with your new employees.

Talk about Relationships

Help them build relationships, and they're more likely to stay. Fill their "lunch cards" for at least the first two weeks. In your early, ongoing conversations, you might ask questions like these:

★   What kind of support or direction do you need from me that you aren't getting? What are you getting that you don't want?

★   How are you getting along with your other team members? What introductions would you like me to make? Are you finding people to go to lunch with? Are you finding people to go to when you need help?

Talk about the Job

They joined your organization because you offered work they love to do. Are they doing it? If the job doesn't measure up to what you promised, find ways to close the gap. Check in early and often—daily in the beginning. These questions should help:

★   How does the job measure up to what we promised so far? Where are we on or off course? How might we correct course?

★   What other interests would you like to explore, either now or over time?

Talk about the Organization

The people you carefully recruited and selected are now onboard. Are they wondering who or what they've joined? Early on, ask questions like these:

★   How does the work pace and schedule work for you? Is there anything we need to adjust?

★   How is our organization the same or different from your last employer? What do you miss most? Least?

★   How can I help you get more of what you want from this workplace? We want you to be happy here!

Yes, all this conversation and connecting requires time and energy on your part. But it might just prevent a quick quit!

→ TRY THIS

★ Introduce new hires to others on your team even before their first day. You might avoid "ghosting"—when someone accepts another offer before reporting to work in *your* organization.

★ Meet with them often: daily for the first few weeks and then at least once a month for the rest of the first year. Build your relationship consistently.

★ Have an "expectations exchange" with your new (and existing) employees. Clearly define what you expect from them and ask what they are expecting from you.

★ Spend time teaching them about the organization they have just joined. Tell stories, sharing your experiences and knowledge about the culture and history.

★ Involve your key people in the new hires' orientation. Expose new employees to others' views as well as your own.

Be available to support new hires in this uncertain early stage of their employment. That may mean seeking them out to see how they are doing and conveying that you are behind them all the way.

Rerecruit as Well

But what about the rest of your talent? While you are busy hiring the best-fit candidates for key roles on your team, do a little rerecruiting along the way. Often candidates and new employees are viewed as close to perfect, and they get all the attention. If you have done a great job of selecting, you will have a whole new collection of stars. Your long-term employees can feel less noticed, less appreciated, and perhaps even taken for granted as you carefully select, orient, and train these new folks. Avoid that dangerous phenomenon by rerecruiting *all* your talent. Show your current employees that they are important and critical to you and to the success of your team, especially as you recruit new team members.

If you're not recruiting your best people,
you're the only one who isn't.

They Are Choosing Too

A much sought-after new hire, when explaining how he chose which offer to select, said, "They put me first. They asked, 'What do you want to do?' 'What are your ideas?' and so on."

Be aware that today's tech-savvy, talented candidates are well prepared and have many choices. Imagine that they arrive with a grid in their heads (or on their smartphones) that might look like table 8.2. This grid helps the candidate ask you questions, evaluate the opportunity somewhat objectively, and compare yours with other job opportunities.

Table 8.2. Candidate's evaluation of job opportunities

CANDIDATES' WANTS / NEEDS	YOUR ORGANIZATION	YOUR COMPETITOR	ANOTHER JOB
Fair pay			
Great boss			
Awesome team			
Flexibility			
Massages on Fridays			

Be prepared to *sell* your organization or team to candidates by addressing the key issues they raise. Treat candidates more like customers than subordinates. Think carefully about what you and your team can offer and be ready to give specific examples. Whatever your unique selling proposition, recognize it and leverage it during the interview.

Beware: don't oversell. Often an employee's exit is due to unrealistic expectations of the job and organization. If the recruitment process is honest and open, you can avoid the quick exit.

ALAS

I've left a few companies after being there only a few months. In a couple of cases, the projects turned out much less interesting or challenging than management had described. In one case, I was told about a system that would have been really interesting, but once I got there and actually started talking with them about the details, I found out that the things they described to me weren't possible technically. Another time, as a contractor, I was brought in to do software development. Instead, they put me on production support. When my contract was up three months later, I chose, to their dismay, not to continue the contract.

—Software engineer

H

If You Manage Managers

Engagement and retention start with the hiring process. Help the managers you manage do a better job of choosing talent. Consider a training course for how to select the best candidates, collaborate to create interview guides for the next job opening, and join them in the next interview they conduct. Debrief the experience afterward and help them fine-tune their approaches.

BOTTOM LINE

Great managers are great recruiters. The best never take down their "Help Wanted" sign. If you get the right people in the right roles in your organization and on your team, you absolutely will increase the odds of retaining them. And don't ever stop rerecruiting your key talent. Remember, your competitors want the talent you've worked so hard to hire.

CHAPTER NINE

Information

SHARE IT

Ponder this: Information—do you have it? Hoard it?

In the information age, powerful new businesses exist solely to lead you to the information you want. That reality has changed people's attitudes toward having, sharing, or hoarding information.

> *The Web will change relationships with employees. We will never again have discussions where knowledge is hidden in some-body's pocket. You will have to lead with ideas, not by controlling information.*
>
> —Jack Welch, former CEO, General Electric

Jack Welch's prediction has come true.

What if you don't share information?

First: It's hard for you to do your best without good information. The same is true for your employees.

Second: You will lose your talent—maybe not today, but eventually those with choices will leave you, either physically or psychologically.

What if you *do* share information?
Your talented people will feel included, trusted, and empowered. They'll appreciate you for sharing. And, bottom line, they will be more engaged and will stay longer.

Having the Scoop or Being Out of the Loop

As kids, we knew that having the inside scoop is cool, and we felt important if we had information that others did not have. If information is power, then being out of the loop—lacking information—might leave one powerless. People want a boss with influence and power in the organization. Think about your own work experience, and you will probably agree that you would much rather work for someone who is in the loop than for a boss who is clueless. Your employees are no different. They want you to be in the loop.

They *all* want and need you to bring them in the loop too.

ALAS

My boss claims to want an inclusive culture but fails to include some of us when sharing important information about the company, its challenges, its future. When my teammates get inside info and I don't, I feel excluded . . . not really a part of the team.

—Boomer on a largely millennial team

If you say you are committed to building an inclusive culture, your employees watch for evidence of that. Beware of saying one thing and doing another.

In the Absence of Information, People Will Make It Up

Information sharing during dramatic change is even more critical than during stable times. We have seen dozens of examples of high-level managers deciding to withhold information in organizations going through major change (downsizing, mergers, acquisitions). We've seen middle managers hoarding information out of fear of losing their power or importance. We acknowledge that at times you simply cannot share, but check out what might happen when you withhold information about change:

Senior Manager Thinks	Employees Think
It's too early to tell them.	Silence must mean it's pretty bad.
This news is too frightening—we'd better wait.	They're moving the company to Panama.
I'm afraid if we tell them, productivity will drop.	The company's going belly-up. Where else can I get a job?

Notice that the manager is trying to protect the employees and prevent all the chatter that can put a huge dent in productivity. Ironically, the silence and protection backfire. Productivity plummets as these employees worry about their jobs and update their résumés.

In contrast, where top leaders give information as early and honestly as possible and hold managers accountable for passing the news down, employees actually feel important and valued, minimizing the productivity dip.

Another good reason to share information is that your employees might be able to help. A major hospital offers a good example:

The hospital had a policy of never eliminating positions through layoffs—a commitment it had kept throughout its history, including its merger with another hospital. Several years ago, the policy was tested when the hospital faced a potential $20 million deficit. Management shared the news with the staff and asked for their help. Within 10 days, managers received 4,000 cost-saving ideas from employees. Sixteen task forces formed to deal with the ideas. While most of the strategies involved tighter controls on purchasing, employees also suggested forgoing raises and holding off on accrued paid time off. By the end of the year, the task forces had realized enough savings to eliminate the need for layoffs.

Giving Your Fair Share

Love 'em managers share more! They share openly, honestly, and often. What about you? How do you know what and how much to share?

To some degree it depends on your organization's culture and management philosophy. At one end of the openness continuum lies the philosophy of "open book management," a set of beliefs and business practices that dozens of highly successful organizations have adopted. Open book management entails building a company in which everyone has access to the same information: operating metrics, financial data, valuation estimates. This philosophy suggests that the more people understand what's really going on in their company, the more eager they are to help solve its problems.

On the other end of the continuum lie more secretive, sometimes even strongly paternalistic cultures. A participant in a training program in Asia told us that in his organization, managers are more like parents, who need to protect and care for their children. They might tell overly positive stories about the company and downplay threats and upcoming changes—all in the attempt to shield people from the news.

Consider the consequences of your communication style, the culture you come from, and the culture in which you manage. Do what you can to share information with your employees in ways that work best for them. You'll increase commitment and enhance the odds of keeping your best people.

No, You Don't Need a Crystal Ball

Your team expects you to help them look to the future. That includes providing information that supports your employees' development. You need to share what you know about the following:

★ Your organization's strategic direction and goals

★ Your profession's, industry's, and organization's future

★ The emerging trends and new developments that may affect career possibilities

★ The cultural and political realities of your organization

As you forecast, your team members will learn to look broadly at their profession, industry, and organization and see the trends and implications. They will also feel more competent and confident in their future marketability.

→ TRY THIS

★ Forward articles about your industry for your employees to read. You might have access to industry-based blogs, newsletters, reports, and magazines that they aren't aware of. Share critical information that can help them make decisions about their career development.

★ State the organization's business strategies and vision—again. If you think that's a waste of your valuable time, think again.

★ Ask your talented people what information they want from you, when they want it, and in what form they'd like to get it. Is it in an email, face-to-face, by phone?

Inquiring Minds

Have you ever had a boss tell you, "I knew that weeks ago but couldn't [or decided not to] share it with you"? Isn't that infuriating? You may have thought, "Thanks a lot. A lot of good this does me now!" or "See if I trust you in the future" or "Why even tell me you knew? Is this a power trip?"

A CEO accepted the resignation of a member of his senior team and knew there would be an impact on the organization. When we asked him when he planned to share that information with his key players, he responded, "I don't want to upset them during a tense time, so I think I'll wait until our staff meeting in two days."

What do you think? Good idea? No, bad idea. What are the odds that people wouldn't find out about the resignation the same day? People knew within the hour and were frustrated, disappointed, and even angry that the CEO had not informed them immediately. Many felt distrusted, even undervalued by their boss as a result of his nondisclosure.

ALAS

We were working on a large government-sponsored program and spent hours preparing for a "proof of concept" demonstration. Meanwhile, our boss was in higher-level discussions with the client and learned that the entire program was going through a funding review. The plug might be pulled before the demonstration took place. We didn't hear about it until the day of the demonstration. Then we learned how close we had come to the demonstration never taking place. We felt disenfranchised and undervalued. Had he shared the seriousness of the situation with us, we could have alleviated his worry that much sooner.

Our boss probably thought he was shielding us from things we didn't need to worry about, or he thought we wouldn't give 100 percent if we knew about this conversation. He didn't place much value on our ability to contribute. After that, my trust level with my manager was never the same. I think the whole team felt the same way.

—Senior engineer, large engineering research institute

So, as a manager, when should you share information?

The sooner the better! When you are clear about what you want or need to share, find a way to do it soon, especially if the information is about a major change. Here are some *trigger events* that might alert you to the need for information giving:

★   A merger or acquisition

★   An online or print article about the company

★   A requisition for a key position

★   New hires

★   An overactive rumor mill

How to Share

Remember that the primary focus of this book is how to keep your talented employees. Volumes have been written about communication strategies, in both normal times and during dramatic change. Face-to-face communication, social media, videos, newsletters, blogs, email, voice mail, all-hands meetings, YouTube videos, and bulletin boards all have their place in communicating effectively. Our question is, which approach works best, given your organization's culture and the message you are trying to send?

Here are some guidelines:

Share information face-to-face, especially if it is difficult to deliver or will affect your employees significantly. Tell your direct reports the news yourself, rather than having them learn it via email or from some other source. Let your supervisors give the news to their direct reports also. Research shows that people believe it and react more favorably when the news comes from their direct supervisor.

★ Get creative. The more creatively you send a message, the greater the chance your employees will notice it. Consider doing the unexpected. If people are used to hearing news via email, try face-to-face or video delivery next time.

★ If the news has to travel through several layers, do a "transmission check." Find out if your message is accurately getting through.

Close to the Vest?

Building an information-rich culture can be challenging. After all, there will be times when you have information that you simply cannot share. A few simple guidelines can help you handle these situations appropriately without alienating your employees. When you must hold information in confidence, keep these tips in mind:

★ Never use information withholding as a power tool. If you receive proprietary or "secret" information, do not tell people you have it unless they ask you.

★ If people ask you if you have information, be honest. Tell them that you are not at liberty to share, and tell them why. For example, you could say, "The information is sensitive or proprietary" or "I have been asked to keep it confidential, and I need to honor that request."

★ Be prepared for the possibility that your responses may not please people. If you establish a track record of early, honest information sharing, you will have more room to withhold information when you must.

It's a Two-Way Street

Getting information is also a way of keeping your employees. Your job is to share it *and* to seek it! People want to be heard regarding their jobs, the work at hand, and the organization's goals and strategies. As a manager, you need to ask for that input.

> *When I started visiting the plants and meeting with employees, the tremendous, positive energy in our conversations was reassuring. One man said he had been with the company for 25 years and hated every minute of it—until he was asked for his opinion. He said that question transformed his job.*
>
> —VP in a global pharmaceutical company

While most managers expect employees to come to them if there is a problem, often employees don't feel comfortable or managers don't offer the opportunity. Take differences into account as you ask for information. In some cultures, employees wouldn't consider giving the boss bad news. Include every member of your team in ongoing information exchanges; find ways that really work for each person.

Too Much of a Good Thing?

Do you ever feel like there's just too much information coming your way?

> *Where is the life we have lost in living?*
> *Where is the wisdom we have lost in knowledge?*
> *Where is the knowledge we have lost in information?*
>
> —T. S. Eliot, *The Rock*

What? T. S. Eliot felt the same way you feel?

The information avalanche causes some workers to say they're reaching a breaking point. They feel demoralized when they can't manage all the information that comes their way at work. What can you do to relieve that stress? Ask your employees if they're getting enough or too much information from you or from their colleagues. Brainstorm solutions with the teams you manage. Establish agreements with them about how to increase effectiveness by decreasing the quantity and increasing the quality of information flowing their way.

If You Manage Managers

How well are your managers handling information sharing? Do a "transmission check" to make sure the key points are getting through to the people they manage. Hold them accountable for accurate, timely information sharing. Their employees' job performance and satisfaction depend on it.

BOTTOM LINE

Information is a form of currency on the job. How you spend it and how you acquire it has a big impact on your ability to engage and retain talented people. Stay in the loop, and keep your employees in the loop. It will help you keep your talent.

Jerk
DON'T BE ONE

Ponder this: Who is the jerk at work?

—WARNING—
If this book landed on your desk
with a bookmark here, pay attention!

Have you ever had a boss who exhibited "jerklike" behaviors? You know, they're the ones who shout, humiliate, discriminate, fail to listen, demand perfection, show disrespect, betray trust, simply don't care—and the list goes on. How did you feel? What did you do?

And if the word *jerk* doesn't exactly translate for you, how about one of the words in figure 10.1?

Figure 10.1. Are you one?

In Greek, we hear, there are at least 20 words that mean "jerk."

No matter what the name for it is, people in every culture and in every company occasionally, sometimes accidentally, exhibit jerklike behaviors. Georgetown University professor Christine Porath found that 98 percent of the workers surveyed over the past 20 years have experienced rude boss behavior, and 99 percent have witnessed it. And the situation seems to be worsening, as civility in the workplace declines.[1]

People cautioned us not to write this chapter, or at least not to use this title. But to avoid this topic is to avoid discussing a primary reason why people leave their jobs. If employees don't like their bosses, they will leave even when they are well paid, receive recognition, and have a chance to learn and grow. In fact, disliking the boss is one of the top causes of talent loss. Take a look at this exit interview:

> **Interviewer:** *Gerardo, why have you decided to leave the organization? I know that we pay competitively and you just received a bonus.*
>
> **Gerardo:** *Is this confidential?*
>
> **Interviewer:** *Definitely, yes.*
>
> **Gerardo:** *The pay is fine. The work is fine. But my boss is impossible. He is so difficult to work with, and I've decided life is too short to spend it working for a jerk.*

Have you ever worked for a jerk? Are there any jerks in your organization?

We've received dozens of jerk stories from our readers. The list was so long, it became downright depressing. Here are just a few examples:

ALAS AFTER ALAS

"My boss told me to come talk to him anytime. I went in for a topic important to me: my career. He kept reading (even answering) his email while I talked. Guess how important I felt."

"The boss I refer to as 'Mr. Toxic' mocked my accent and food choices. He even suggested I get help to reduce my accent so that I would 'fit in' better."

> *"Prior to a meeting my boss said, 'You take charge, run the meeting, assert your authority.' During the meeting, the boss continually interrupted, contradicted, and undermined my authority, even though I followed our preset agenda."*
>
> *"The dentist I worked for actually threw instruments at me when I wasn't fast enough in assisting him. Our patients were horrified, and many left our practice because of it."*
>
> *"My boss put two talented employees on a 30-day suspension because they left work to go home and check on their kids immediately following a 7.0 earthquake in Seattle. He, by the way, had already checked in with his wife and knew his kids were fine."*

Hard to believe? Maybe not. Unfortunately, most of us have worked for a jerk at some point in our lives. Most of us escaped!

This chapter is not about labeling people as jerks and letting the rest of us off the hook. It is about defining jerklike behaviors and the "jerk mode" that people occasionally assume. It is about learning to assess whether you exhibit those behaviors and how often. And it's about trying to change for the better. Why? To engage, motivate, and keep your talented people.

What Is a Jerk?

We asked dozens of people, "What do jerks act like or look like?" This checklist reflects what we heard. We dare you to score yourself.

→ TRY THIS

Instructions: Score yourself on the following behaviors, using a 0–5 scale: 0 means you never act this way, and 5 means you often act this way.

How often do you	0–5
Intimidate	_____
Discriminate	_____
Condescend or demean	_____
Act arrogant	_____

How often do you	0–5
Slam doors, pound tables	————
Swear	————
Behave rudely	————
Belittle people in front of others	————
Micromanage	————
Manage up, not down	————
Always look out for number one	————
Give mostly negative feedback	————
Yell at people	————
Tell lies or "half-truths"	————
Act above the rules	————
Enjoy making people sweat	————
Act superior to or smarter than everyone else	————
Show disrespect	————
Act sexist	————
Act prejudiced	————
Use inappropriate humor	————
Blow up in meetings	————
Start every sentence with "I"	————
Steal credit or the spotlight from others	————
Block career moves (prevent promotion or keep "stars")	————
Distrust most people	————
Show favoritism	————
Humiliate and embarrass others	————
Criticize often (at a personal level)	————
Overuse sarcasm	————
Sexually harass	————
Deliberately ignore or isolate some people	————
Set impossible goals or deadlines	————

How often do you   0–5

Betray trust or confidences   _____

Undermine authority   _____

Gossip/spread rumors   _____

Act as if others are stupid   _____

Have "sloppy moods" (when feeling down,
take it out on others)   _____

Use fear as a motivator   _____

Show revenge   _____

Interrupt constantly   _____

Make "bad taste" remarks   _____

Demand perfection   _____

Break promises   _____

Second-guess constantly   _____

Have to always be in control   _____

Mock others about accents, food choices, clothing   _____

Sins of Omission (not the things you do but the things
you forget or fail to do)

How often do you   0–5

Withhold praise   _____

Withhold critical information   _____

Fail to truly care   _____

Forget to ask what they need or want   _____

Fail to listen   _____

Lack patience   _____

Fail to accept blame, let others take the hit   _____

                                  Total score: _____

Note: This is an insight tool meant to help you evaluate which of these
behaviors you might occasionally, accidentally exhibit. The following
interpretation guidelines are just that—guidelines.

Interpretation Guidelines

0–20	Although you have a bad day now and then, you are probably not viewed as a jerk. Watch those behaviors for which you scored above a 3, and get more feedback from your employees.
21–60	Look out! You could be viewed as a jerk by some, at least in some situations. Commit to identifying and working on your jerklike behaviors.
61 or more	You are at high risk for losing talent. Get more feedback and get some help (maybe a coach).

If you gave yourself a score of 0 on all the behaviors in this assessment, you might be a saint. In other words, most of us do exhibit some of these behaviors some of the time. The question is, how many and how often? And what effect does your behavior have on the people who report to you? Often, leaders are the last to know that their style is off-putting. Watch for drops in productivity, difficulty hiring, lateral moves out of your department, and, of course, turnover.

Look at your results through an inclusion lens. How do your unconscious biases factor into the equation? Do you tend to exhibit more jerklike behaviors with those who are different from you? Are you more civil to those who look, talk, vote, eat, and smell like you?

Note: Many jerklike behaviors fit perfectly into definitions of *bullying*, especially emotional bullying. Regardless of the labels, the effect is the same. People with options will simply not put up with jerklike or bullying behavior for long. They will leave you, psychologically or physically.

Consider the Cost

Toxic leaders can become liabilities when they exhibit jerklike behavior. From headaches to heart attacks, the stress of working for a jerk takes a toll on employees. The financial costs mount as absenteeism, disability claims, medical leaves, and lawsuits increase. And what about the emotional, psychological side of this equation? Could you be ruining your employees' marriages? It may sound extreme, but think about the last time you felt beat up at work and headed home to spill the nastiness all over your family. You get the picture.

Who, Me?

We spend a lot of time teaching leaders what to do. We don't spend enough time teaching leaders what to stop. Half the leaders I have met don't need to learn what to do. They need to learn what to stop.

—Peter Drucker, management expert

Give your results from the jerk checklist some serious thought. Ask your friends at work to look at the list with you and give you honest feedback. (If you don't have any friends, that may be a clue.) Ask family members to give you insight as well. If others agree that you *often* exhibit more than one or two of those behaviors, you are at high risk for losing talent.

Jerklike behaviors are so damaging that even one or two can negate all your other strengths as a boss.

I had no idea that my employees viewed me as such a jerk. We had 360-degree feedback (input from boss, peers, subordinates, even customers) as a part of a leadership development program. Employees had a chance to type in comments at the end of a lengthy computerized survey. My employees basically told me that I came across as insensitive and uncaring. They said that my drive to get results seemed to be at any cost, including employee health and morale. I was so shocked at this feedback. I felt terrible. Now I'm working with a coach to help me figure out how to change my behaviors. The first step was finding out how my employees viewed me.

—Senior manager, engineering firm

If you have never had an in-depth 360-degree feedback assessment, consider it. The feedback should come to you anonymously, and you should use it for your own awareness and development. Recognizing your ineffective and potentially damaging behaviors is the first step to doing something about them.

Once a Jerk, Always a Jerk?

Just as you can learn new leadership skills at any age, you can stop ineffective behaviors or replace them with more effective ones.

> I used to blow up at people. When I was under stress, and some-
> one said the wrong thing, I just lost control. I yelled, turned red
> in the face, and pounded the table. The result was that people
> used to tiptoe around me. They hid bad news and took few risks,
> fearing my temper if they failed. People were intimidated. We
> lost creativity, productivity, and some talent along the way—
> all because of my uncontrolled temper.
>
> Now I'm better, at least 90 percent of the time. It took some
> time and a lot of effort, but I now have a handle on my emotions.
> When I feel the blood pressure rise and my anger coming on, I
> picture a stop sign. I stop; I take three slow, deep breaths; and
> then we talk about the problem. What a difference—both in how
> I feel about myself and how my employees react.
>
> —Manager, marketing and sales department

Because behaviors are learned, we know that it is possible to change. It may not be easy, but it is possible. The difficulty of changing ineffective behaviors depends on the answers to several questions:

★ How ingrained is the behavior? Have you been acting this way for 50 years or for 3? Some of those long-term habits are certainly more difficult to break than those you learned more recently.

★ Are you crystal-clear about what the desired behavior will look like? A clear picture of the goal will certainly make it easier to get there.

★ Do you have resources available to help you? It's easier to change if you have people supporting you.

★ How complex is the behavior? You may be able to decide simply to stop telling off-color jokes and never do it again. Negative reactions under stress are more complicated and interwoven, so they will probably require more focus, more resources, and a longer time to change. You may need to develop a new repertoire of behaviors.

★ Do you really want to change? Why? If you can't answer this question, you will not change. You've got to want to.

Once you decide to change, you can create your action plan.

What might you do to reduce your jerklike behaviors? First, get honest feedback. You need a clear picture of how you look to others. Then ask yourself, "So what?" Think about the implications of your behaviors. Are they getting in the way of your effectiveness? Are they causing good people to leave? Consider a stress management course. Exercise. Eat well. Sleep more. Try tai chi, yoga, meditation, or prayer.

If you decide to change, seek help from others. You could get a coach or counselor, attend a personal growth seminar, or read a good self-improvement book. And remember to ask people to monitor your behavior and give you feedback as you work to change.

Be patient with yourself and with others. It takes time to change behaviors. And it takes time for others to trust you—especially if you've exhibited jerklike behaviors for a long time.

If You Manage Managers

A colleague said, "You need to can them or coach them!" People watch to see how you deal with the jerks you manage. Mentor them, manage their performance, and get them some help. If they continue their jerklike behavior, move them out of management.

BOTTOM LINE

If you believe (or find out) that you often exhibit jerklike behaviors, decide to change. This entire book exists to help you do it. Changing jerklike behaviors may be the most important action you can take to keep your talent on your team.

CHAPTER ELEVEN

icks

GET SOME

Ponder this: How often do they smile? How often do you smile?

How do you feel about fun at work? Do you believe in it? Have it? Support it? Make it happen? Discourage it? Evaluate your own assumptions about fun at work. Then consider creating and supporting kicks in the workplace as one way to keep your best people.

Research shows that a fun-filled workplace generates enthusiasm—and that enthusiasm leads to increased productivity, better customer service, a positive attitude about the company, and higher odds that your talent will stay.

Fun for One—Fun for All?

> *If we are hungry for fun, we are "starved" for fun at work.*
> —Leslie Yerkes, **author of** *301 Ways to Have Fun at Work*

When was the last time you had fun at work? Last year? Last month? Last week? Yesterday? If your answer was yesterday, you're probably smiling as you read this.

Of course, one person's fun can be another person's turnoff.

Telling jokes may be fun for you and ridiculous (or even insulting) to someone else. Some people get kicks out of decorating your office as a birthday surprise, while others love to take a break to debate some current hot topic or to surf the web. So remember to ask people, "What makes work more fun?"

Cultures can vary greatly in their definition of fun. Taking your team to a local fair and the dunk tank could be a kick for some and

93

a nightmare for others. Privately ask every member of your diverse team what works best for them. And never target someone's ethnicity, accent, or food choices—even if you think, "It doesn't bother him."

Fun-Free Zone

Unfortunately, many workplaces are fun-free zones. If your employees were to grade you on the degree to which you support fun at work, what would you get? If you say, "I'd get a C+," why is that? Maybe you just were not raised that way. The bosses you learned from may have been fun-averse, serious taskmasters. Perhaps you believe that allowing fun at work will cause you to lose control or fail to achieve results. You might think that moments of levity will set bad precedents and that the group will never get back to business. Some of your concerns may be based on *fun myths* about having kicks in the workplace.

→ TRY THIS

Check which of these myths you tend to believe:

★ Myth 1: Professionalism and fun are incompatible.

★ Myth 2: It takes toys and money to have fun at work.

★ Myth 3: Fun means laughter.

★ Myth 4: You have to plan for fun.

★ Myth 5: Fun time at work will compromise results.

★ Myth 6: You have to have a good sense of humor (or be funny) to create a fun work environment.

Myth Debunking

These myths are just that. Let's debunk them.

Myth 1: Professionalism and Fun Are Incompatible

Can you have fun and still maintain a professional work environment? It depends on the kind of fun you are talking about. Slapstick silliness (pie-in-the-face humor) will not fit well in a business-suit environment. But there are many appropriate ways to get some kicks in even the most buttoned-up workplace.

Every month we had client reports due and most of us dreaded the solitary extra-hours work that the task required. So we started planning to stay late one night each month. We went to a deli for snacks and good wine and then held a work party. We were all on our own computers in our own offices, but we took regular breaks, helped each other, enjoyed our food and wine together, and had some laughs in the after-work casual environment. It not only made the monthly task much more enjoyable, but it provided a type of team building.

—Consultant, management consulting firm

In another highly professional work environment, when someone is late to a meeting, the person either has to sing a song or tell a new joke (in good taste!). People are on time more often since the new rule was implemented, but there is also a guaranteed chuckle as people slide in the door a minute or two late.

Most of the concern about having fun in a serious workplace is actually concern about inappropriate humor, loud behavior, or poor timing. If employees' timing is off or their behavior is embarrassing or disruptive, give them that feedback, just as you would about any work behaviors. Having fun at work might actually be an acquired skill for some people. You can help them get better at it!

Myth 2: It Takes Toys and Money to Have Fun at Work

Myth 2 is the sister myth to "It takes toys and money to have fun in life." When we asked dozens of people to reflect on fun times they remembered having at work, here is what we heard. (Notice how many of these examples cost money or involve toys.)

★ "No specific time. It was just the day-to-day laughter my colleagues and I shared—mostly about small things."

★ "We decorated my boss's office for his birthday. We used five bags of confetti from the shredding machine."

★ "Spontaneous after-work trips to the local pizza parlor."

★ "When we had a huge project, a tight deadline, and we had to work all night. I wouldn't want to do that often, but we had a good time, laughs in the middle of the night, and a thrill when we finished the project."

★ "Receiving this poem from my dedicated, funny employees whom
I sent to Detroit on business: 'Roses are red, violets are blue, it's
30 below, and we hate you.'"

Toys and money certainly can help you have fun too. Many global
companies have "fun" budgets. In those companies, people are expected
to work hard and play hard. Their play includes the occasional extrav-
agant party or boat trip. Although employees greatly appreciate elab-
orate outings, most report that it is the day-to-day work environment
that matters most. It has to be enjoyable.

Myth 3: Fun Means Laughter

Fun often does involve laughter or smiles. Sometimes people just need
to take themselves less seriously. Laughter has been called *internal
jogging*, as it has the same positive health benefit as an aerobic run.
Supposedly this works through the release of endorphins, the healing
elements of the body. And even better, you can lose four pounds of fat
a year by laughing an additional 15 minutes a day!

Did you know: Kids laugh, on average, 400 times per day—adults,
12. Hang out with a seven-year-old for a day and count.

But people can have fun at work without laughing or getting silly.

*In my company we are more formal and serious. You might call
our form of kicks serious fun. We enjoy celebration and together-
ness at the end of a project, during Chinese New Year, on family
days, or during team exercise or department meals out.*

—Colleague in Singapore

An intriguing project and collaboration with wonderful teammates can truly be fun. Work that is meaningful and makes a difference can be fun. Building something new can be fun.

*Some of the most fun I ever had was in the early days of creating
a completely new form of airplane. We were building something
new that would make a difference. It was difficult and challenging
but so much fun.*

—Retired aeronautical engineer

Myth 4: You Have to Plan for Fun

Planned fun makes sense sometimes. The employee softball team provides fun and requires planning, as does an occasional employee picnic or the annual holiday party. But a lot of fun in the workplace is spontaneous.

> *We had been working so hard and had nailed all our goals for the quarter. My boss called us into his office and presented the team with movie tickets—for the two o'clock show that day! It was great. We took off as a group and felt like kids, playing hooky from school. It was so spontaneous and so appreciated.*
>
> —City government employee

Unplanned fun can be as simple as showing up at the staff meeting with muffins for everyone, asking a group of employees to join you for lunch at a new restaurant, or taking an unplanned coffee break to just sit and talk about families or hobbies.

K

Myth 5: Fun Time at Work Will Compromise Results

Many managers are concerned that every minute spent chuckling is a minute lost toward bottom-line results.

ALAS

Somehow three of us stepped out of our offices at the same time, met in the hallway, and began chatting. I don't even remember what we began laughing about, but all three of us were really laughing (not very quietly). Our boss stepped out of his office with a furious, red-faced look and said, "Is this what I'm paying you for?" We were embarrassed, humiliated, and angry. I left the company shortly after that, as did the other two people. It was a stifling environment where fun was not allowed. Ten years later, I still remember that incident.

—Retail sales manager

Fun-loving environments are actually more productive than their humorless counterparts. A fun break can reenergize your employees and ready them for the next concentrated effort. In one Microsoft group, employees take breaks whenever they want by surfing the web or playing games on their computers. They say that these playful activities clear their minds so that when they return to the project at hand, they are fresher and sharper.

> *We have a tradition of celebrating birthdays. We recently celebrated the birthday of our financial officer with a special morning tea. We always sing happy birthday, share a funny story or two, and chat over tea and cake. Yes, it's a chunk of time out of the morning, but we've had a few laughs, our financial officer has been valued (and he truly is!), and everybody goes back to work.*
> —Matt Hawkins, New Zealand ministry

You might be thinking, "If I allow my employees to surf the web or celebrate birthdays during work, they will never get their work done." Maybe you believe that only exceptional employees can be trusted to that degree. The secret to allowing fun at work is to be *crystal clear* with your employees about their performance goals. Cocreate measurable and specific goals with them; then evaluate their performance using those goals.

Some of the most productive, successful organizations in the world are renowned for fun. The late Southwest Airlines chairman of the board, Herb Kelleher, set the famous Southwest tone. He loaded baggage on Thanksgiving Day, rode his Harley-Davidson motorcycle into company headquarters, and golfed at the Southwest golf tournament with just one club. He even arm wrestled another CEO for the rights to an advertising slogan.

> *If you aren't having fun in your work, fix the problem before it becomes serious: ask for help if you need it. If you can't fix it and won't ask for help, please go away before you spoil the fun for the rest of us.*
> —Russ Walden, founder, Father's Heart Ministry

Myth 6: You Have to Have a Good Sense of Humor (or Be Funny) to Create a Fun Work Environment

Some of you aren't funny. Well, you aren't. And that's okay. Many terrific bosses are not necessarily funny (or even very fun-loving). In many cases, they simply allow others' humor and playfulness to come out. They support rather than create fun at work. Let others initiate the kicks if fun is not your strength.

> *Our national director recently did something very unusual (for him) at our monthly strategy meeting. He asked each of us whether we preferred Coke or Pepsi. Depending on our answer, he pulled a Coke or Pepsi out of this bag. He never does things like that. It was a riot!*
>
> —Employee from a nonprofit organization in Russia

You might bring fun into your workplace by having brown-bag lunches with interesting speakers and topics. During a hobby-sharing lunch, one employee took everyone to a local park to demonstrate his remote-controlled airplanes. Another brought a local merchant to give a session on wine tasting. Another invited the local golf pro to give everyone a lesson.

> *Fun is a state of mind. Leaders can create this state of mind—but to do so, they must care about people, show trust and apprecia-tion, be humble enough to join in, and believe it is a good use of time! Joy is the lasting by-product of having fun and being with folks who give you energy. Leaders can bring joy to people's lives, even when things are tough. Creating a sense of being a part of something very special is the key.*
>
> —President of a major airline company

If You Manage Managers

How are the managers you manage doing in the "fun" department? How fun are you to report to? Model the behaviors you want from them. One senior leader we met brought his leaders together to dis-cuss and "test-drive" a list of fun activities for the department. Expect leaders to *allow* fun to happen on their teams. Do not let them be fun squelchers!

BOTTOM LINE

Experience in companies of all sizes proves it: fun enhances creativity, fosters commitment, improves morale, mends conflicts, and creates effective customer relationships. It enhances workplace productivity when work goals are clear. Let fun happen. That fun will energize, motivate, and keep talented people on your team.

CHAPTER TWELVE

Link

CREATE CONNECTIONS

Ponder this: Is your organization easy to leave?

It's *easy* to leave a workplace if you

★ Feel no connection

★ Have no group of colleagues who can offer support, information, or plain old gripe sessions

★ Do not have relationships that help you get your work done

★ Don't look forward to seeing the people with whom you interact

★ Don't feel proud of or don't understand the organization's mission and purpose

It's *difficult* to leave a workplace when you have links (connections) to *people* and organizational *purpose*. On some level you know that's true. But are you helping your talented people create the links that will engage and retain them?

Are You a Linker or Nonlinker?

A *nonlinker* thinks, "If I connect my employees to other functions or departments, someone there will steal them."

A *linker* thinks, "If I don't connect my employees to other functions or departments, their knowledge and skills are less likely to grow. My employees' productivity will be limited to the resources of their own department. Their work may become too function focused for overall success, and I won't be as connected as I need to be, either."

Just as we are each positioned at the center of our own particular universe, each of us is also positioned at the center of our network. We realize, of course, that all other people are positioned at the center of their networks, and that is as it should be.

Each of the people in any given network serves as a source of support (referrals, help, information, etc.) for everyone else in that network.

Those who know how to use the tremendous strength of a network realize this very important fact:

We are not dependent on each other; nor are we independent of each other; we are all interdependent with each other.
        —Bob Burg, author of *Endless Referrals*

To increase performance *and* retention, consider how you can support connections between your employees, the organizational purpose, and other people.

Link to People

Do you have a best friend at work? What a strange question to ask (especially in some countries and cultures). What does the answer have to do with employee engagement or retention? According to Gallup, a lot![1] Research shows that strong relationships at work are absolutely key to retaining your people and key to their productivity. In fact, most of us want and need colleagues to think with, work with, and create with. This is true with virtual teams as well.

What if you work in London and your team is in Kansas? Hundreds of thousands of employees and their bosses work in virtual environments. They've created dozens of ways of building and maintaining their relationships, despite geographic differences.

ALAS

The competition offered me a 10 percent salary increase, and I took it. My boss was blown away by my resignation. He thought I loved my job and had no idea that I could be enticed away. So what grabbed me?

Frankly, it was a combination of things. I felt no real connection to my workplace or the team. Maybe if we had spent a little more time together, or I had felt more a part of things there, I might have stayed. The company I'm joining operates primarily in teams. I'm hoping that will provide more of the interaction that I'm looking for. So the money was attractive, but the chance to be part of a team mattered even more.

—Engineer, aerospace firm

Most workers want to be linked to a group of people with whom they enjoy working. In fact, for the newest generation entering the workforce, the number one question on their minds may be, "Will I work with a team I like?" This is so true that they will even leave together. We heard recently of 13 IT employees resigning as a group!

Work atmosphere is the main reason I stay. We have an amazing teamwork philosophy. In fact, it doesn't matter where in the country I am. I can stop at any retail dealership and say, "Hi, I'm a fuel service engineer," and I'm immediately welcomed. It feels great to be part of a family like that.

—Gas station owner

Leverage ERGs

In the past two decades, employee resource groups (ERGs, previously called affinity groups) and business resource groups (BRGs) have proved they are business assets by demonstrating their value in recruitment and retention, marketing, brand enhancement, training, and employee development. Top managers of some companies began to view their ERG/BRGs as instrumental to the success of their businesses. This opinion is proliferating as corporations become more global and populations and workforces more diverse.

Encourage your employees to build their networks by joining (or starting) professional and social groups inside your organization. When employees have connections based on a shared affinity, they are more likely to feel valued and engaged. That bodes well for increased retention. ERG/BRGs give leaders a path to understanding and reacting to a demographic group's concerns. Leaders linked to talent via these groups deepen their ability to engage and retain traditionally underrepresented talent.

ERG/BRGs also help people break out of silos and create cross-department connections. That in turn can increase innovation, invite fresh new problem-solving ideas, and create long-lasting friendships and collaboration. And you know where that can lead: increased engagement and retention.

One global organization proudly boasts 54 ERG/BRGs! Here are just a few we've heard of:

★ Gender, racial, ethnic groups

★ Young professionals

★ Veterans

★ Non–US born

★ Faith based

★ Gays, lesbians, bisexuals, transgender people, and allies

★ Parents or work-life

★ Early career

★ People with disabilities

★ Generational (boomers, Xers, Ys, Zs)

★ Women in leadership

★ Introverted leaders

★ New employees

★ Pet owners

★ Curly-haired people (not kidding!)

You name it, the ERG/BRG exists somewhere in an organization led by managers or individual contributors who are smart enough to know the value of connecting.

One manager said she was opposed to the ERG/BRG concept, fearing it would create cliques or tribes, leaving people out. We've observed that the benefits of these groups outweigh the risks. They provide a warm welcome for younger workers, who are quick to leave a workplace where they feel they don't readily belong. Similarly, talented people from other circumstances, ethnicities, countries, and cultures find comfort and encouragement from those that are *like them* in some way and with whom they can therefore easily relate.

In Asia, many organizations have "Friends@Work" committees that plan social events for employees. These are funded by the company to help build relationships. They also have volunteer committees, where employees get together for an outing with the elderly, handicapped people, or disadvantaged children. This links them to the community and to one another.

Supporting connections with people throughout your organization can help you attract and keep prized employees. Here are some ideas:

→ TRY THIS

★ Use your company intranet to help boost team collaboration, find organizational resources, and acknowledge and celebrate successes.

★ Reinstate *lunch*. (Kudos to you if it still exists in your organization.) Encourage people to enjoy it together.

★ Encourage teams, task forces, and ERG/BRGs, where people form new connections and new friendships. Sponsor a departmental sports team, or have sports outings with other departments or companies.

★ At the next staff meeting, encourage team members who belong to ERG/BRGs to share with the larger group what they are doing and what they enjoy about it.

★ Have family events, such as picnics, bring-the-kids-to-work day, or bring-your-dogs-to-work day.

Link to Purpose

You don't need to work for the American Red Cross or the Bill & Melinda Gates Foundation to build a meaningful connection between an employee and the organization. As a manager, you can do a lot to create the link. Sometimes all it takes is a discussion about the history of the company, its founders, its reason for being, the important needs it meets, or what customers say the company has done for them through its product line or service.

One surgical device manufacturer brought in patients from a local hospital whose lives were saved or enhanced thanks to the company's product. All employees at all levels attended these meetings and were able to ask questions of these users. Employees swelled with pride and deepened their link to the organization.

Meetings with the president, CEO, or other senior leaders are critical to linking employees with an organization's purpose. While mission statements capture the underlying principles of the organization and seldom change, the goals of the organization are dynamic. Keep employees abreast of these organization-wide changes to help them feel connected.

How do you create a strong link between your talented people and the organization and its purpose? There are many ways:

→ TRY THIS

★ Have regular open-forum meetings. If employees feel they are being heard, they will feel a stronger connection to you and the group. Allow diverse opinions and disagreement on the way to finding solutions that work.

★ Give employees time to talk. Managers are often so worried about work not getting done that they discourage personal conversations among their staff. What they don't seem to understand is that these conversations help employees feel connected to each other. And ironically, they're often talking about work!

★ Host informal breakfasts or lunches. In a semisocial atmosphere, you can introduce a new project, get creative juices flowing, or just kick off a new month. One senior manager gave lunch coupons to the 60 employees in his unit three times a year. There was only one instruction each time: "Take someone you don't know well to lunch, and learn more about them and the work they do."

★ List all the interdepartmental meetings you attend in a week. (Does the list give you a headache?) Which ones could you delegate to members of your team? The linking could be great for them and freeing for you.

Purpose beyond the Organization

Getting your employees involved in community service can help them feel connected. For some, these activities are a major reason for choosing one organization over the next or staying with their present one.

Don't despair if your organization is not yet involved in socially responsible activities in the community. You can support community projects your employees are involved in. Or you might build your own. Either way, promoting a cause within your department or company gives employees a sense of pride, promotes teamwork, fosters a bond among employees, and provides skill development as well. Companies have involved their employees in classrooms, community centers, charity runs, bicycle tours, public housing projects, outreach to the elderly, and many other life-changing activities.

Every year, my company sponsors several hundred cyclists in a ride called the Best Buddies Challenge. My colleagues and I train for months for this event, have a wonderful time doing it, and help raise millions of dollars for the charity. The best part of it all is knowing we've supported a global volunteer movement that creates opportunities for one-to-one friendships, employment, and leadership development for people with intellectual and developmental disabilities. I'm proud to be a part of a company that supports community activities like this one!

—Staffing director, investment bank

If you're wondering what you might do to support this kind of purpose, consider these possibilities:

➜ TRY THIS

★ Investigate local projects, discuss them at a staff meeting, and ask who's interested.

★ Ask employees to suggest projects, and select one or two (or more) a year to work on as a group.

★ Invite several local volunteer groups to describe what they are doing in the community, and encourage your team to volunteer together.

★ Invite another department to join with you on a local community project (great networking for your employees).

Link, and Let Them In on the Secret of Reciprocity

The Latin expression *quid pro quo* means "something for something" or, in a more contemporary translation, "If you do something for me, I'll do something for you." If linking is used only to ask something of others, it will become one-sided and self-serving.

We like the phrase "elegant currencies"—things you can offer that are easy for you to do that the other person needs but lacks resources to do. For example, you can teach somebody a new computer program. You can tell someone about a book you've read that could be invaluable to his or her work or even summarize it for him or her. There are so many ways that people can offer something in return.

Consider your quid pro quo menu. Which services can you offer as a thank-you?

★   Introduce links to others

★   Provide original ideas

★   Help others brainstorm

★   Volunteer help

★   Increase others' networks

★   Reduce others' workloads

★   Offer feedback

★   Recommend to others

★   Share expertise

Direct reciprocity doesn't have to be the only way this works. The idea of *paying it forward* suggests that individuals offer to "give back" by giving to three other people. Eventually, we'd all win. Imagine an organization that plays out this philosophy. Perhaps you could begin this in your own department. Ask your employees how they can pay it forward to colleagues, to their profession, to their community, to their organization, perhaps even to their industry.

If You Manage Managers

If the leaders who report to you are nonlinkers, help them learn to reach out. Their new connections can certainly help them but will also provide a crucial network for their talented employees to tap into. It may seem counterintuitive, but it's true that people are more likely to stay and produce when they're surrounded and supported by many.

BOTTOM LINE

Connections are a major reason people say they stay with organizations. If links are weak or nonexistent, disengaging or leaving is easier. Today's knowledge workers need to link to others to get their jobs done. Their links will strengthen yours—in the ideal quid pro quo—and they'll be more likely to stay.

CHAPTER THIRTEEN

Mentor

BE ONE

Ponder this: What are they really learning from you?

People with mentors are more likely to stay. And they won't just stay longer, they'll produce more.

Mentoring has become a way not only to transfer crucial skills and knowledge but to inspire loyalty in new employees, emerging leaders, and older workers who might otherwise leave sooner. It also broadens the opportunity net to include those who might have been overlooked. If you hope to build a more inclusive organization, consider mentoring as one powerful approach to doing that.

Companies are giving creative incentives to mentors, pairing mentors with new hires, and offering group mentoring and online mentoring to hasten the development of management and technical skills. They're even linking diverse cultures by pairing mentors with their mentees across the globe.

But this book is not about structured mentoring programs that HR professionals put in place. This is about the mentoring that you can do, from your position as a manager, now. And it's not that complex. The more you act like a mentor to your direct reports, the more engaged they'll be. The more engaged they are, the less they'll think about leaving.

I had just finished a presentation to a large group of high potential employees and their leaders and was waiting in the lobby of the hotel for my ride to the airport. I watched as two gentlemen from the group briskly walked over to one another and exchanged

a big, warm bear hug. I was intrigued since the group was quite
formal, so I walked over and asked how they knew one another.
They said, almost in unison, that they were mentor and mentee.
Always curious, I asked the mentee what made his mentor so
great. He said, without skipping a beat, "He was authentic."
Then I asked the mentor what made his mentee so special
and he said (also without skipping a beat), "He was hungry."

—Bev Kaye

So What's a Mentor to Do?

Mentoring does not require specific training or a great deal of time. Every good manager mentors naturally, often without even realizing it. When you think about mentoring, think about these three practices:

★ Walk your talk.

★ Guide from the side.

★ Tell it like it is.

Walk Your Talk

Model what you want your employees to do. Help them find other good role models as well.

An executive I coached said he encouraged his employees to have
work-life balance—that it was crucial to their health, well-being,
and job effectiveness. I asked him how he modeled that for his
employees. There was dead silence on the phone. Finally, he
admitted, "I guess I don't really model that." It turned out his
car was the first one in the parking lot every day and the last
one to leave. His family rarely saw him. What was the effect on
his employees? They paid more attention to what he did than
to what he said. It was clear to them that work-life balance was
not—and should not be—a priority.

—Executive coach

So, how effectively are you modeling the behaviors you hope your employees will replicate? Harvard professor Rosabeth Moss Kanter says that modeling needs to be dynamic, not subtle. It requires *follow-me* behavior that is obvious and noticeable.

If you want employees to exhibit work-life balance, demonstrate how you do it, in obvious, consistent ways. If you hope they'll be better listeners, be a terrific listener every time you interact with them.

If you want your talented people to delegate more effectively, delegate more effectively to them. If you want them to be continuous learners, talk about the online course you're taking to improve your skills in a specific area. You get the point.

How are *you* modeling in a day-to-day way? Here are some ideas:

→ TRY THIS

★ Be aware of what you are modeling—is it what you hope to see employees doing?

★ Point out other good role models. Choose people who are good at the very things your employees are trying to learn.

★ Be authentic. Let them see you handling good and bad situations, under positive conditions and poor ones.

★ Discuss what you're trying to model. Is it coming through? Admit when your attempt falls short and ask how you might improve.

M

Guide from the Side

Find out where employees need more support—then give it. Cheer them on, in good times and bad.

Show you care about them and their unique skills and capabilities.

Sometimes, all that is required of a mentor is pure encouragement. In our hectic, robust lives, it is often the most neglected of all mentor roles.

Encouragement is all in the eye of the perceiver. For example, an employee says, "He never encouraged me," while her manager says, "I encouraged her all the time." How can you encourage effectively?

Clearly, attention and retention go hand in hand.

My boss moves away from his computer and phone, to a small round table, for every one of our weekly conversations. I feel like the most important person on the planet. He listens, asks great questions, gives advice, takes his time—even though I know how busy he is. I'd follow this boss to the ends of the earth!
—Manager, global restaurant chain

Those who *have* been encouraged are more likely to stay and to bring their best to the team.

Some managers encourage naturally, through casual conversations. Here's one way of offering encouragement, just in time. It consists of three steps:

1. **Recognize:** Notice something.

2. **Verbalize:** Say something.

3. **Mobilize:** Do something.

Any of the three steps will encourage, but all three combined are much more powerful. For example, Liliana gives a beautifully designed flyer to her manager and says, "I've been doing some fiddling with that new graphics program."

Recognize. Manager: "Hmm, looks great. I didn't know you like this kind of stuff."

Recognize and Verbalize. Manager: "This is really good. Is this something you'd like to do more of ?"

Recognize, Verbalize, and Mobilize. Manager: "If you like this kind of work, why not let Marc in graphics know, and while you're there, find out when he's offering his next graphics course."

→ TRY THIS

★ Remember to encourage employees when things don't go as well as planned. If you're there for them during the good times and bad, they'll trust you, perform for you, and stick around a while longer.

★ Encourage risk-taking that is essential to growth. Take the culture into account as you do this!

★ Cheer them on. Give regular positive feedback—and developmental feedback too.

Countless employees who have left their corporations say that their managers never stopped long enough to understand them or care about them.

ALAS

From an interview with a senior-level manager in a high-tech company:

Interviewer: *Did you ever have a mentor?*

Manager: *You bet. He was my manager. He really cared about me. He'd stop in all the time, ask me some great questions, get me to think about what I was doing and why. He gave me some great strokes and kept my juices flowing.*

Interviewer: *Do you do that for anyone?*

Manager: *No—I would like to, but we don't really have the time these days.*

Mentoring takes time—but not a lot. Mainly, it takes a willingness to show another person that you genuinely care.

Nurture others' ideas. When employees come to you with suggestions or ideas about how they might approach something differently, do you immediately say no? We hear that employees feel put down and turned down far more than their managers are aware. And that makes leaving easier. Instead, try listening to the entire idea, try playing with it as a "what if." Ask for more information. Listen to understand; many people just want to be heard.

Nurture relationships. Get to know your employees and give them every opportunity to get to know you—personally as well as professionally. The more differences you have with an employee, the more important this step is.

Mentoring expert Wendy Axelrod points out that when you have a mentee whose world is very different from your own, you need to be tuned in and open. Consider it part of your job description, not the other way around. Gaining cultural awareness and valuing differences opens up your thinking, helps you check your assumptions, and makes you aware of unconscious biases. You become more available to your mentees and more appreciative of them.

As you learn more about your employees, let them know more about you.

I'll never forget my manager trusting his team enough to share his story. He said he had been working too hard. He knew it but did nothing about it. One day he was walking up the stairs at work and stopped—unable to go either up or down. Something was terribly wrong. He was hospitalized with a nervous breakdown and missed weeks of work. He learned a lesson that he hoped his employees could learn, too: don't let work hurt your life. The team was riveted. His story had a huge impact on all of us.

—IT team member

Help your talented people build relationships with others in the organization too. Those connections will help them get their work done and increase the odds they'll stay.

→ TRY THIS

★ Show you care about your talented people and their unique skills, talents, capabilities—even their personal lives.

★ Link them to others who can help them grow.

★ Listen to their ideas with an open mind. Think, "What if?" before you think, "No."

Tell It Like It Is

Help employees avoid those organizational minefields that are never written about in any policy manual.

Everyone knows at least one sad story of a technically brilliant employee with everything to offer who derailed because of political blunders, lack of interpersonal skills, or ignorance of the unwritten rules. Countless corporate advice books suggest that academic brilliance alone does not lead to success. Daniel Goleman talks about EQ (emotional quotient—your ability to monitor your own and others' feelings).[1] Paul Stoltz refers to AQ (adversity quotient—your ability to deal with bad luck or plans gone wrong).[2] Others point to arrogance, insensitivity to others, or managing up instead of down (focusing more on superiors than on direct reports) as career stoppers.

These experts also mention that career stoppers in one organization are not necessarily stoppers in another. Arrogance might derail a talented employee on your team, while it's seen as a success factor somewhere else. The key here is to help your employees learn what works (and what doesn't) in *this* organization. Your ability and willingness to *tell it like it is* can save a career, perhaps for the benefit of your own organization.

ALAS

She was technically brilliant. She graduated in the top 2 percent of her class in one of the top schools in the country. She was pursued by all our competitors. We won. We offered opportunities for her to continue on her fast track. She was so quick, though, that she started to rub people the wrong way. She continually ignored our chain of command. No one gave her any alternative ways to deal with the folks whose respect she needed.

Slowly, her influence eroded. Although she continued to be technically brilliant, she just couldn't manage to effectively communicate with her team or her peers. People avoided her. She became more isolated and more unhappy. Before we knew enough to try to talk it out and give her some help, we lost her.

—Manager, high-tech company

This employee's style and interpersonal skills might have worked just great in school or even in another organization. They didn't work here, given this company's culture. And no one told her.

Good mentoring can mean telling an employee that her actions could derail her in this company. Listen to the voice in your head that says, "That behavior isn't going to work here." It can also mean telling her which meetings she dare not be late for—or which managers she dare not go around. It's sharing news about the unwritten rules, about how the organization looks to you and how it behaves—often.

But what if you coach someone about organization politics and you are wrong? Your view is just your view. Could you mess it up even more? We don't think so.

We have never heard of a manager who mentored too much and thereby lost an employee. We've never heard of a manager who coached too often and thereby lost someone's trust. We've never heard of a manager who talked too frequently about how he or she saw the organizational world and failed to retain talent for that reason.

Employees need to know your point of view. They want to know your take on how people get and give resources, what kinds of influence strategies work and don't work, and what certain senior leaders want and don't want in their reports, their presentations, and their meetings. And they want to know this before they walk into a minefield. At the very least, they want to be able to look at something that didn't work and understand why.

So if you are nodding your head, consider using one of your own staff meetings to open a dialogue on organizational reality.

→ TRY THIS

Invite your team to talk about any of the following topics:

★ What have I learned about what counts in this organization?

★ How have my failures and successes contributed to my growth?

★ What most surprised me about the culture?

★ What was the most difficult culture shift for me to make?

★ What are the ways to get in really hot water here?

★ How do people derail themselves?

★ What do I know now that I wish I had known then?

People have a hunger for frank conversation in organizations today. Because of the intense competition, few employees feel that they can really express themselves or ask the questions that are on their minds. Most people claim they do not like playing politics. But because it's a reality of corporate life, a mentor watches out for a protégé's organizational well-being. A mentor educates a protégé and helps prevent him or her from stumbling.

Following a seminar, we received this letter from one of the participants:

One of my mentors made a big difference in my career. We had spent weeks working together on the development plan for one of my stars. When we finished the last discussion and agreed it would work, I looked at him and said, "Done." I slumped back in

*my chair and took a relief-filled breath. I was happy we had cre-
ated a solution. I looked around my desk and saw all the pending
projects and piled up papers and said, "Boy, I'm glad that's over.
Now we can get back to work."*

*He looked at me and said, "You don't understand, Joe; this is our
work. If we don't do this, we have nothing. This is our job."*

Now there's a mentor.

Help Them Find Many Mentors

Today, your talented employees will seldom be matched up with one
senior, savvy person who is supposed to know it all and can teach it to
them. Instead, you can help them find many mentors. These mentors
could include a tech-savvy person two cubicles down, a colleague with
niche knowledge, or a senior manager willing to have lunch and chat
about top-level leadership. Interactions could entail minutes, hours,
months, or years, depending on what works best for both mentor and
mentee. Today's mentor has the exciting opportunity to help different
people in different ways.

Mentor in Reverse

What do you want to learn? Who on your team (or beyond) can teach
you how to use social media to your advantage? Who's a dynamite pre-
senter who could teach you some platform skills? Who could help you
become a more effective networker?

Let your people mentor you. Let them tell you what they know. Ask
them to coach you about how you might be more effective. They'll feel
valued and respected because you asked.

If You Manage Managers

As you mentor managers, ask how they're mentoring their employees.
Tell them honestly what you see them modeling (the good and the not
so good) and brainstorm ideas for improvement. Ask them for feedback about your mentoring skills—in what ways do they hope you'll
get even better at this vital task?

BOTTOM LINE

Your employees want you to teach them the ropes, and they know their careers will suffer if you don't. Your failures and your success stories provide valuable insights that just don't come in other ways. They want you to model the behaviors you expect from them. Managers who mentor establish great rapport with their employees and find that there is a strong payback in engagement and retention.

CHAPTER FOURTEEN

Numbers

RUN THEM

Ponder this: What is the real cost of talent loss?

Who is your talent? They are your high-fliers, high-potentials, and stars. They're also your solid citizens—the ones who show up every day to do great work. They are men and women, young and old. They look, speak, create, and think differently from you. And you need them on your team. Calculate the cost of losing any or all of them, and then consider how you'll keep them—for at least a little while longer.

Imagine that you arrive at work one morning to evidence of a burglary. A brand-new computer has disappeared from an employee's desk. You call the building security office and the police. Then you launch your own investigation. You are determined to find out how this happened and who is responsible. You will not rest until the case is solved. And you immediately increase security measures—no more property will be lost.

Now think about the last time one of your most talented employees was stolen by the competition or just walked out your door. What kind of investigation did you launch? What measures did you implement to prevent it from happening again? Maybe the loss of this precious asset set off no alarm bells because no one ever really assessed the cost of losing talent. It doesn't take long to run the numbers. And you may be surprised by the result.

Numbers and financial statements are the universal language of business. Frontline workers and senior managers alike understand them. We'll be speaking of US dollars here, but many of our clients are counting in euros, pesos, pounds, rupees, or one of another 180-plus global currencies.

We're not just losing good people; we're losing great people. Almost one in every five of the people who leave us voluntarily every year is a top performer. The cost of this turnover in lost productivity, paperwork, recruitment, and training is huge— it's in the tens of millions of dollars.

—COO, international bank

A careful assessment of the numbers might just convince you to focus more sharply on retaining your talent.

What's the Price Tag?

It's cheaper to keep her.

—Spoken by a classroom participant

You may think these dedicated, talented people who have been critical to your success are easily replaced. And yes, you might even find replacements at lower salaries. We hear this argument often, especially during periods of high unemployment when many good people are looking for work. Often, though, the managers who say this have simply not calculated the real costs of turnover. Most experts agree that replacing a key person on your staff will cost you two times that person's annual compensation. "Platinum" workers (highly skilled professionals) could easily cost you four to five times their annual salaries.

ALAS

An aerospace firm senior leader described the cost of losing a key member of the organization:

John was one of our most talented engineers and was responsible for inventing some of our key technology. After a phenomenally successful year, he expected some kind of reward or recognition from his boss. When nothing was offered (not even a thank-you), he met with his boss and asked for a 15 percent raise (about $15,000). His boss immediately said, "Forget it!" John did and left the organization to join a competitor who was thrilled to pay him 30 percent more than he had been making. Some said, "Oh, well, we'll replace him within weeks."

Here's what actually happened:

- *We hired a search firm for $50,000 to try to steal someone like John from a competitor.*
- *After a three-month search, we found five good candidates and flew them all in for interviews at a total cost of $20,000.*
- *We selected the new guy (after much wining, dining, and selling) and agreed to a sign-on bonus of $20,000 and a moving allowance of $30,000. His salary was negotiated at 25 percent above John's ($25,000 difference in the first year).*

So the bottom line in salary and expenses looked like about $145,000 to get the new guy in the door. But wait—that's not all.

- *Our competitor won John (including his brilliant brain and technical knowledge) and went on to win a multibillion-dollar contract that would have been ours.*
- *John's buddies all started looking around, and the company executives got wind of it. Senior leadership decided to give them a 15 percent raise for two years in a row (at a cost of $250,000).*
- *We lost two or three other key people to competitors. Their technical expertise went with them. Our cutting-edge technology leaked out the doors, and we made our competition stronger almost overnight.*

So it wasn't a $145,000 cost after all. It was literally multimillions. And this does not take into account the harder-to-measure costs of lowered morale, discontent, and lowered productivity following John's departure. In hindsight, it is clear that his boss (and others) should have worked a little harder to keep John. They should have recognized him, paid him what he was worth in the market, and also made certain that he was challenged and happy with his day-to-day work. Losing him was a very costly mistake.

—Manager, global aerospace company

This true story may seem unusual. Certainly not every employee is worth millions to your bottom line. However, no one, other than the manager in this story, ran the numbers to figure out what losing John actually cost. Managers seldom do because then they would have to look for the real causes of turnover or find somewhere to place blame. They might even need to create retention strategies. Most leaders just don't want to do all that.

Some readers have reacted to this story by saying, "Hey, wait a minute. John left for more money. We thought you said it's seldom about money!"

Even in this story, his departure was not really about the money. It was about being heard, being appreciated, and being valued. John was hurt and frustrated by a boss who did not recognize or reward his efforts and who immediately dismissed his request for a raise. So what could John's boss have done differently? He could have

★ Praised and thanked John for his major contributions

★ Listened to John's request and acknowledged that he was worth the raise—and that he would see what could be done and by when

★ Asked John what else he could do (if not an immediate raise) to reward him for his contributions

★ Calculated the cost of keeping John ($15,000) compared with the cost of losing him (you saw it—millions!)

You will never really know what it costs to lose a talented employee if you never calculate the cost.

With the real cost of losing talent in mind, we recommend using table 14.1 to assess the cost of replacing one of your excellent employees. We have left blanks for you to add items that are relevant in your organization.

Notice that some of the costs in the table are *direct* and easy to measure, while the remaining costs are *hidden* and more difficult to measure, such as overload on the team and lost customers or business (opportunity costs). Ironically, some of the hidden costs are the highest. Have you calculated those?

Table 14.1. Run the numbers

DIRECT COSTS	COST
Newspaper/internet/social media ads	
Search firm	
Referral bonuses	
Interview costs: airlines, hotels, meals, etc.	
Larger salary, sign-on bonus, or other perks	
Moving allowance	

HIDDEN COSTS	COST
Employee's lost productivity prior to leaving (disengagement; résumé update; time on job search sites; time spent interviewing, negotiating, and accepting new job)	
Work put on hold until replacement is on board	
Overload on team, including overtime to get work done during selection and training of replacement	
Lost customers	
Lost contracts or business	
Lowered morale and productivity	
Loss in business continuity across departmental boundaries and resulting lowered productivity	
Loss of other employees (They follow each other!)	
_____	
_____	
_____	

	COST
Total estimated cost of losing one key employee	

N

What If They "Quit" and Stay?

Have you ever had a job where you brought less than your full self to work every day? What did it cost your organization?

According to a recent *State of the Global Workplace* report, 85 percent of employees are not engaged or are actively disengaged at work.[1] You're better off when they call in sick. The economic consequences of this global norm are approximately $7 trillion in lost productivity. So, while we know that physical turnover costs you a bundle, we now know, too, that psychological turnover can cost as much or more.

The good news is that what engages people also keeps them.

Consider this:

★ How much money would your organization save if it reduced regrettable turnover by 1 percent? How would your organization use those dollars if they did not have to be spent on recruiting, hiring, and training new employees?

> *We ran the numbers. We would save $91 million by reducing regrettable turnover by 1 percent. We'd been talking about how much we (store managers) all wanted the latest high-tech copy machine, but the $200,000 price tag made it a dream, not a possibility. We laughed when one manager did the calculation and announced we could buy 455 of these machines (plenty to go around) if we could just hang on to our talent!*
> —FedEx Office Print & Ship Center,
> management meeting

★ How much could your organization make if talented people brought 5 percent more of their hearts and heads to work? What could you do with that money?

If You Manage Managers

Devote one staff meeting to the cost of loss. Have each of your managers think about the recent loss of one talented individual and calculate the actual cost of that loss. Encourage and incent your managers to reduce regrettable turnover, just as you expect (and inspect) every other cost-cutting measure in your organization.

BOTTOM LINE

Run the numbers. Calculate the costs of losing and replacing key talent. Assessing these costs can be eye-opening for managers with an "easy come, easy go" attitude toward turnover. Sharpen your commitment to keeping your most valuable employees fully engaged and on your team.

N

CHAPTER FIFTEEN

Opportunities

MINE THEM

Ponder this: How opportunity-rich is your organization?

What does this say?

OPPORTUNITY ISNOWHERE

The optimists among you read, *Opportunity is now here!*

The pessimists see, *Opportunity is nowhere.*

Still others of you are pretty sure it says *Opportunity I snow here* (and we'd like to meet with you later).

While this exercise usually brings a chuckle, it also underscores the truth about your employees and their perceptions about what's possible in your organization. Some scan the horizon and see absolutely no opportunities to learn or grow or be challenged. Others scan the same horizon and see an opportunity-rich environment. They envision possibility where others see nothing. What accounts for the difference? Often, *it's the manager.*

Love 'em managers help *all* their employees find great next-step opportunities. These engagement-focused managers listen carefully to the diverse requests their talented people bring them. They avoid pigeonholing and making assumptions about what opportunities people would really want.

Learn how to "opportunity mine" with the people you count on to stay and to bring their best to work every single day.

ALAS

Lindsay was a rising star, destined to do great things for the team—and her excellent work always made her supervisor look terrific. When she gave notice and her manager asked why, she answered, "I've been very happy here. You're a fantastic boss and the people are wonderful. It's just that I'm ready for something new, and this opportunity popped up in another company. I wasn't really looking for it; it just happened. I've decided to go for it."

The manager felt absolutely sick about losing her. What on earth would the team do? He offered more money, but the lure of this new, exciting opportunity had her already mentally and emotionally out the door. And when the manager probed a bit, he realized that the very opportunity she was leaving for was available within the organization. Imagine if he had shared such opportunities in staff meetings, where everyone could hear them.

Responsibility rests on both sides. Lindsay didn't ask, and her manager didn't offer to help her look for the next opportunity.

"I'm leaving for a better opportunity." That's the most common answer to the most popular exit interview question, "Why are you leaving?" Sometimes it's just the politically savvy thing to say (rather than saying "My boss was a jerk"), and sometimes it's the truth. Talented people have many choices about where they work. To keep them engaged and in your organization, learn how to "opportunity mine" with them.

Opportunity mining means opportunism in the most positive sense of the word. As the name suggests, it entails digging deeply, looking carefully, and ultimately capturing the new opportunity. Its three key behaviors are *seeking*, *seeing*, and *seizing*. As a manager, you can partner with your employees to opportunity mine. Begin by getting a feel for your own level of opportunity-mindedness. Complete the Opportunity Audit to find out if you are *opportunity-high* or *opportunity-shy*.

Opportunity Audit

Using the following scale, jot down the number that best indicates the extent to which each statement is true for you:

1 = RARELY; 2 = SOMETIMES; 3 = USUALLY; 4 = ALWAYS

_____ I am at ease when considering other people's viewpoints.

_____ I seek and use new technologies for improving productivity.

_____ I know the trends in the marketplace; I could tell you what competitors are doing and why.

_____ I take an active role in professional groups.

_____ I network to help launch and support my career growth.

_____ I am flexible about adjusting plans when the first or second attempt at something fails.

_____ I am quite comfortable interpreting the gray areas of policy and practices.

_____ I let my career interests be known through formal (job posting) and informal (conversation) channels.

_____ I know how to connect people and information, and others seek my help in gaining access or information.

How did you do? If you are opportunity-high (scoring over 27), you are probably already seeking, seeing, and seizing opportunities for yourself and maybe even with and for your employees. If you scored on the low end (anything less than 18), you might benefit from the suggestions that follow. Only the opportunity-minded manager can truly help employees find possibilities for themselves.

There is no security on this earth; there is only opportunity.

—General Douglas MacArthur

Seeking Opportunities

People who seek opportunities often see the glint of something new— and can follow through for themselves _and_ for their people. Your willingness to seek will model this positive action for your employees. _It's important for you as well._

Do you ever ask employees about the types of opportunities they might be looking for and even help them look? (Yes, even if it means some good folks leave your team.)

One engineering firm is an opportunity-rich organization where managers are opportunity seekers. They have developed a culture where employees feel comfortable speaking up when they are getting bored or need or want a new challenge, a promotion, or a different type of work. Managers hold regular employee development meetings to discuss their employees' interests and desires. They surface new possibilities and link employee goals with opportunities that already exist or are on the horizon. After several years, the results are measurable and positive. Not only do they retain their talented people, but they also have enhanced recruitment, as interviewees see the company as an opportunity-rich organization.

While this company launched its system-wide approach formally, you don't have to do it that way. You can do it yourself.

Hold development meetings with your employees. Your only topic should be their careers and what opportunities they might be seeking. "What if there are no opportunities here?" you ask. "And what if I simply cannot help them or by opening the conversation, I encourage them to leave?" To answer these tough questions, put yourself in their shoes. How do you feel about a boss who wants to help you seek opportunities for yourself? What happens to your level of respect and commitment while you work for him or her? What happens to your sense of loyalty to this boss and even to the team or company? It all goes *up*!

→ TRY THIS

★ Ask your employees what opportunities they seek. Help them think broadly and creatively, going beyond some of the first-blush responses such as a promotion. For example, ask what they'd like to learn this year.

★ Brainstorm to find enrichment opportunities in employees' current jobs.

★ Check with managers in other departments to find out where new possibilities lie.

And remember: You (and they) won't see it till you seek it.

Be aware that some people are opportunity-minded but come from a culture where seeking new opportunities, inside or outside the organization, is viewed as disloyal. Support their exploration: let them know you not only accept it but encourage it and they will not pay a price for doing it.

Seeing Opportunities

To discover opportunities, one must look at the world in a new way, through a new lens. It is impossible to make people smarter, but you can help them see with new eyes.

Turn back to the first page of this chapter. What did you see? Opportunity is now here? Opportunity is nowhere?

Most of us immediately lock on to one perspective and remain fairly confident in our findings. You may have chosen the first answer or the second and did not even consider the possibility that there is another point of view. Try this with your people. It is a great opener for a discussion about opportunities.

If you are an opportunity-minded manager, you will help your employees *seek* opportunities but will also help them to *see* those opportunities when they are right in front of their faces.

I can see how an important learning assignment a manager once gave me positioned me as an expert that others look up to. I was invisible before. I now understand how important it is for me to do the same for my direct reports.

—Manager, high-tech Zimbabwe firm

You can shed the right light, point out the features and distinctions, and look at the opportunity from another angle. Best yet, you will teach your employees how to do those things for themselves. In partnership with your employees, ask, "Where and how carefully are we looking?"

A manufacturing company has an insiders' network of more than 360 people across the organization who are willing to take the time to talk with employees who want to learn about the nature of their work and the requirements of their jobs. This network has a computerized database (called Internal Information Interview Network) with the names and backgrounds of all the employees who participate.

Another organization we know of holds internal career fairs. The message to their talented people is that if they're looking for a new opportunity, they can look inside first!

What great ways to share information about opportunities. And what great ways to see if a pasture that looks greener on the other side of the fence really is greener. If your organization doesn't have databases or internal career fairs, you can still encourage folks who are wondering (and wandering) to interview or email people you know in other areas. Some managers let employees see opportunities by allowing them to fill in for others on vacation or sabbatical. Could you do this?

→ TRY THIS

★ Look around to see what is changing in your department, division, or organization. What new projects are on the horizon?

★ Notice which department is expanding and which one is shrinking. There could be a perfect opportunity in a growing segment of your organization.

★ Who might be retiring soon or leaving for a new opportunity, opening up a possibility for one of your stars?

Seizing Opportunities

Many people are quite good at both seeking and seeing even camouflaged opportunities. But many of us are not so good at the most crucial behavior of the opportunity-minded person: seizing. For example, you may know someone who has a list of stocks or property she *almost* bought, a sport he *almost* learned, or a trip she *almost* took.

If you scored opportunity-high on the Opportunity Audit, you probably seek, see, and seize quite well. If you want to retain your top talent, help them learn to seize opportunities that come their way. What are the barriers to seizing opportunities? It may be helpful to figure out why your employees fail to act and what you might do to help them.

→ TRY THIS

★ If your employees do not create an action plan for their careers, help them analyze why they don't, and then help them do it. These plans should have action steps with timelines, potential obstacles, and support needed.

★ If your employees do not adhere to their plans (they are too busy, resources are delayed), you could help them. Suggest regular meetings to discuss their progress, and brainstorm solutions to obstacles.

★ If your employees second-guess themselves (analysis paralysis), you could help them avoid this pattern. With their agreement, point out second-guessing behaviors that are more apt to be delay tactics than true assessment.

★ If your employees decide a particular opportunity is just not for them, you could help them decide if it truly is not the right choice. After careful assessment, some opportunities are best passed by.

★ If your employees let others talk them out of an opportunity, you could help them be strong in the face of naysayers and risk-averse "friends" and colleagues. Those people may be opportunity-shy.

★ If your employees are afraid to act, you could help them face the fear and just do it! Sometimes we just need an ally to provide support and courage when we get the jitters. Talk about the what-ifs with them—what if you try it and it doesn't work out? Usually the risks are not really life-threatening, even though they may feel like it.

There are two ways to get to the top of an oak tree. One way is to sit on an acorn and wait; the other way is to climb it.
—Kemmons Wilson, founder, Holiday Inn Hotels

They Might Go

If you really love them, you have to be willing to lose them—to their next great opportunity. You might lose them from your team but save them for the enterprise. Or they could find what they're looking for in a new company or country. They might start a business or join a band. In any case, they'll remember how you helped them grow and even how you helped them go with an *elegant exit*. They'll be your ambassador and sing your praises. They'll send new business and talent your way. They might even boomerang back someday.

If You Manage Managers

The managers you manage may not be opportunity mining with their talented people. Why? Because they're afraid of losing their best people. An Amazon.com executive said, "We hire ambitious people. If we don't help them grow here—soon—we'll lose them." There you have it. Hold your managers accountable for opportunity mining with *their* talent, just as you do with them.

BOTTOM LINE

Our research shows that, more than any other single factor, opportunities to be challenged, to do meaningful work, and to learn are what persuade people to stay.

Opportunists often get a bad rap. But if you hope to keep your talent on your team, you must become opportunity-minded—an *opportunist* in the positive sense of the word—on behalf of your people. If they come to you wanting something new or something more, partner with them to find opportunities. Be glad that you have ambitious opportunity miners on your team.

CHAPTER SIXTEEN

Passion
ENCOURAGE IT

Ponder this: When did they last say, "I love my job"?

What do your talented people love most about their jobs? And what are you doing to help them do more of the work they're passionate about and less of the work they dislike?

Passion for work means that people find what they do to be so exciting that it sometimes doesn't even feel like work—so exciting that it brings exhilaration, a "high." Granted, even those who have this passion seldom have it every day, but they do know that feeling, and they know when they lose it. Those who love their work are most engaged and most likely to stay on your team.

Choose a job you love, and you'll never have to work a day in your life.

—Confucius

Passion by Any Other Name

Manager: "Nancy, what's your passion?"

Nancy: "I don't have a passion. I'm an accountant."

The words *love* and *passion* could be favorites for some and a turn-off for others. That's diversity for you. Nancy does have passion for her work but wouldn't use that word. Try something else: "What work do you really enjoy?" or "What do you find most meaningful at work? or "What have you liked best about previous jobs?" or "Are you doing what you choose to do?" (This question came from a colleague in Singapore, where the word *passion* doesn't quite capture the concept.)

As your employees answer, dig a little deeper. Then think creatively about how you might put their passions to work.

In the closing remarks of his book *What Should I Do with My Life?* Po Bronson tells the story of being invited by Michael Dell of Dell Computer to participate on a panel at a gathering of the Business Council, a group of more than 100 CEOs from some of the biggest companies in the country. The panel was asked a great question: "What do employees want? What would it take to get more commitment out of them, more ideas out of them, more value out of them?"

Bronson answered this way:

> *They want to find work they're passionate about. Offering benefits and incentives are mere compromises. Educating people is important but not enough—far too many of our most educated people are operating at quarter-speed, unsure of their place in the world, contributing too little to the productive engine of modern civilization, still feeling like observers, like they haven't come close to living up to their potential. Our guidance needs to be better. We need to encourage people to find their sweet spot. Productivity explodes when people love what they do.*[1]

Sweet Spots

Do you know what your employees' sweet spots are? When we asked dozens of people about their work passions, here is some of what we heard:

★ "I love creating something new, something no one has even imagined before."

★ "I get a kick out of working on such an elite team. There is so much brilliance here."

★ "I love drawing, welding, building something."

★ "I love numbers. I'd rather work with them than with people."

★ "I really get excited when I discover a new rule in math."

★ "I love to help someone get better at something and get happier in the process."

★ "I love managing others. What a kick it is to motivate and guide a team to do great things."

★ "My passion is turnaround—taking something that is broken and fixing it."

★ "I love being part of a great company that is doing important work."

A common theme surfaces among these diverse answers: When people are doing what they love, they are at their best. If you help connect your employees' passions to their jobs, you and they will reap the rewards.

> *Passions are wired into the real world more directly than our workday routines are. If you love something, you'll bring so much of yourself to it that it will create your future.*
>
> —Francis Ford Coppola

Uncover and Discover

When was the last time you pulled your team together to ask for their ideas and to encourage them to build on one another's creativity? When did you sit down with one of your own team members and think together? Employees love the opportunity to think aloud with their managers; they want to "blue sky" occasionally. Do you know who wants this most? Who is most nourished by this kind of interaction? Have you made time for it? Have you made time for the people who crave it?

> *When one manager had the "passion conversation" with his employee, here is how it went:*
>
> Manager: *What do you love to do? What about your work makes you smile?*
>
> Marta: *I've recently learned to use a new piece of graphic software, and I've created brochures for my church. I'm having a ball with it.*
>
> Manager: *I wonder if there is a way we could use your talent and interest here at work.*
>
> Marta: *I've been thinking about it and wondered if I could take on the layout of the new company newsletter we've been talking about.*

Manager: How would that work out with your current heavy workload?

Marta: I will definitely get my work done. You know that about me. This project will be above and beyond my current workload.

Manager: Let's give it a try. Keep me posted as you work on the first issue. Let me know what's working and what's not.

Marta expanded her job to include multiple graphic arts projects. Her boss worked with her to restructure her job so that some of her former duties went to other people. Marta's energy and productivity have soared, and she wakes up eager to go to work. The key to her renewed enthusiasm is that her boss collaborated with her to uncover and then capitalize on her passion.

What if passion lies outside work? Some people are more passionate about skiing or about their children than about their work. What do you do then? Think about how the workplace might allow them to do more of what they love. Working remotely, flextime, and on-site daycare centers are all strategies that support people's passions.

I can't imagine leaving this job. The day-to-day work is good and the team is great. But one of the best aspects of my job is that some of us go skiing most Fridays. We work hard all week to get the work done. We sometimes work evenings and on the weekend when necessary. Then we take off. Skiing is my passion, and this job allows me to enjoy it every week. How many of those jobs are there?

—Accountant, software company

This highly productive employee will continue to produce for his boss and team. That's the payback for his manager's flexibility.

→ TRY THIS

★ Recognize that people have unique passions—different from yours and from their colleagues'.

★ Ask your employees what they love to do. What are they passionate about?

★ Dig deeper. Ask for examples so you really understand what they are saying to you.

★ Get creative. Collaborate with them to find ways to either incorporate their passion into the work they do or flex the schedule to allow time for their passion outside of work.

★ Chat about this important topic at your next staff meeting. Encourage people to help each other increase the passion quotient at work.

Passion Igniters

I asked my employees which part of the day they loved the most. One answered, "Quitting time." Not sure if he was kidding.
—Hardware store manager

When my daughter Lindsey was three, she used to say, "Mom, unbored me."
—Bev Kaye

Are some of your employees bored? Help them get *unbored*. Here are a few passion igniters to consider.

Hire for Passion

Why not select for passion in the first place? Find out if the candidate has a passion for making a difference or for your company's product or service. What about a passion for the work your unit does or for working on a team? Use the answers as engagement clues. If you build a team of passionate people, they'll not only produce for you but actually help retain each other.

> New York Times *journalist and author Thomas Friedman writes about adapting to the ever-changing world of work. He claims, "The winners won't just be those with more I.Q. It will also be those with more P.Q. (passion quotient) and C.Q. (curiosity quotient) . . . to not just learn but to relearn for a lifetime."*[2]

Show *Your* Passion

Share the passion you have for the work with your team. Your actions model what you expect from others.

> *The leader of a fast-growing financial corporation spoke to his regional leaders at a recent conference. When he walked into the room, he received a thunderous standing ovation. His talk was about the challenges and successes of the company—and focused largely on the role of people in the success equation. Midway through his speech, he said, "It's all about product, processes, and people. Without the people, all we have is an empty building— nothing else." In his closing remarks, he said, "I love this com- pany. And I love the people in it!" The place exploded.*

This leader feels passionate about his work and the people he leads. And he's not afraid to show it.

Share a Meaningful Mission

What if you shifted from maximizing profit to maximizing *purpose*? What if you could help employees fall in love with your company's agenda?

Speaking of agenda, what is yours? Why does your team or orga- nization exist? What is your mission? Share that mission with your employees. Then clearly link employees' work to the mission. Tell them how their work contributes to it. Tell them how critical they are to you, to the mission of the team, and to the organization.

> *I've been the janitor and maintenance expert here for 30 years. We take care of older people who need nursing care and help with their daily living. They deserve the best after all they have done and given in their lives. I love my work. I help make this building beautiful and safe for the people who work here and the people who live here. The director here gave me an award for my service and told everyone how critical I am to serving our residents. That award hangs on my wall at home.*
>
> —Maintenance expert, nursing home

This man is crystal-clear about the value of his work. The mission of the organization is the reason for his being there, and it inspires him.

→ TRY THIS

★ Hire passionate people for your team.

★ Provide activities that boost learning and fun.

★ Share and show *your* passion for the work and for the people.

★ Articulate and link people to the mission of your organization or team.

Passion Busters

Sometimes the fire is there at the beginning and it just plain goes out. People with passion can burn out if someone or something smothers their passion. They can also move to a place where their passion can be rekindled.

ALAS

He loved training and teaching others and told me he wanted to do more of that. Every chance he had, he would volunteer to teach a class, any class, even if it wasn't technical training. He learned to facilitate a team-building process that proved to be very successful in his business unit. But I just couldn't free him up to do more of what he loved. He was one of our best engineers, and we couldn't afford to have him pulled off his key projects to do this other work. How silly, in hindsight, that I was so protective of him and his time— now I have neither. He left us six months ago for a job that lets him utilize his talent and passion.

—Director, public service organization

P

Organizational Constraints

Which organizational constraints prevent you from giving your employees different work or more of the kind of work they love? The list is often lengthy. Some people just call the constraints "reality." You might think that in reality we don't have enough of the following:

★ **Time**. We barely have time to do our jobs, let alone help our people find work they love.

★ **Money.** The organization just slashed budgets again. We have no money for extras.

★ **Staff.** We laid off the human resources expert who helped me match employees to meaningful community outreach projects. I don't know how to make those links, even if I had the time.

★ **Management support.** My manager is in the same spot I'm in: not enough time, money, or staff.

★ _____ (fill in the blank)

These constraints may be real. But remember, if you don't help your talented employees find work they love in your organization, you will lose them. Do you have enough time, money, and staff to deal with their loss and replacement?

People Change

Think about it. Do you love the same things you loved 10 years ago? Or do you have some new passions?

Sometimes passion stops because people change. I have a collection of unread books on topics I used to be very interested in—and am not now. Passion found another avenue for expression.

—A reviewer for this book

This is why the stay interview is so important and why you need to have these conversations regularly with anyone you hope to keep on your team. People's passions might change; and when the thrill is gone, they could be too. Ask your talented people what's new. And then explore together what could be new.

Self-Interest

When you help your best employees uncover and pursue their passions, they may need to leave you to pursue those dreams. Out of self-interest (sometimes team interest), you might tend to avoid the passion discussion. Yet your odds of keeping those people are better when you collaborate with them to find exciting, meaningful work right where they are.

> *I found meaning as a volunteer. I spent evenings and weekends with a group that was working with inner-city kids in Los Angeles. We mentored them and provided safe playgrounds and education. When I described how much I loved this work, my boss had a brilliant idea. He said the organization was committing to some new community outreach programs and that they were thinking of creating a new role in the organization. The next thing I knew, I became the director of community projects for our corporation. My work and my passion are now one and the same. As long as I can do this, I will never leave this organization!*
>
> —Director, entertainment company

The boss lost this employee from the team (it was inevitable) but *saved* him—and his passion—for the organization.

→ TRY THIS

★ Assess the organizational constraints that serve as passion busters. Are they real? How can you overcome them?

★ Be honest about your self-interests. Get clear about the costs and benefits of helping employees find work they love.

★ Support and encourage your employees as they change, grow, and exhibit new passion.

If You Manage Managers

Ask your managers, "Do you know what your people are passionate about?" If they answer yes, ask how they're helping their talent get more of that at work. If they answer no, encourage them to find out—to learn what makes their best people jump out of bed in the morning to bring their best to work.

BOTTOM LINE

People who do what they love usually do it very well. If passion is missing at work, your best people may not bring their best *to* work. Collaborate with them to uncover and discover what they love to do—what brings them meaning. Link them and their work to your mission and help them remove the barriers to doing what they love. You'll gain enthusiastic employees who will stay engaged and productive—and *on your team.*

CHAPTER SEVENTEEN

Question

RECONSIDER THE RULES

Ponder this: Which would you rather keep—the rules or the people?

If innovation is so important,

★ Why is it so hard to support?

★ Why is it so easy to say no before saying yes?

★ Why is it easier to see if there is a precedent for what an employee wants to do?

★ Why do we hang on tightly and fail to question a rule?

★ Why do we often say, "We've never done it that way; why start now?"

★ Why do we seldom say, "Rules are meant to be broken"?

When your employees come to you with new ideas, concepts, or rule breakers, they want to hear "You've got a point" or "Let's give it a try" or "Maybe that will work." They want you to (at least occasionally) go to bat for them—to truly advocate for the change they want.

They want you to recognize their good ideas and innovative solutions, and they want *you* to support their questioning. You will increase the odds of engaging and keeping talented employees if you allow them to question the rules about their jobs, the workplace, and even the business.

A Rule's a Rule

The world would be even more chaotic if there were no rules. We count on rules to provide safety and sanity in our communities and workplaces. Yet most of us would agree that progress demands questioning the rules.

What if these people hadn't questioned the rules?

★ Wright Brothers: Why can't people fly?

★ Steve Jobs: Why can't we create phones that are also computers?

★ Thomas Edison: Why can't we light our homes with electricity?

★ Fred Smith: Why can't we move packages across the globe overnight?

★ Jonas Salk: Why can't we prevent polio?

What if others hadn't asked these questions?

★ Why can't we go to the moon?

★ Why can't we use lasers to perform surgery?

★ Why can't we share data instantly over long distances?

★ Why can't we build our social connections online?

★ Why can't we create radar-invisible aircraft and ships?

You get the idea. The rule questioners and ultimately the rule breakers are our innovators. They improve our lives, and they are the backbone of successful organizations.

ALAS

Darren was a new employee, hired to bring us fresh ideas and an outside perspective. He began to annoy us during his first month. He kept asking us questions like "Have you thought about doing it this way?" and "Why does this process take eight steps when it could be four?" We held firmly to the way it had been done—why fix it if it ain't broken? Darren hung in there for six months and then shocked us all by leaving. He said that new ideas were not appreciated here. The sad thing is he's right.

—Manager, global medical technology firm

You might be thinking that Darren could have waited for a few months before suggesting all those changes. But didn't the company hire him in part for his new eyes and fresh ideas? Darren would have thrived in a workplace that truly encourages creativity.

So how open are you to the questions your employees bring you?

→ TRY THIS

Complete the following sentences to determine whether you are more like Manager A or Manager B:

When employees ask me to question the rules, I most often

Manager A	Manager B
☐ Give them a quick yes or no answer	☐ Tell them I would like to explore it further with them
☐ Give them the reasons why we do it this way	☐ Avoid justifying how we currently do it
☐ Tell them I don't have time to deal with it	☐ Suggest a time frame for dealing with their question
☐ Suggest they ask someone else	☐ Collaborate with them to find other resources if necessary

If you are more like Manager A, you may be action oriented and highly productive. While you may have many excellent traits, you also could be a *question-unfriendly manager.* It won't take long for your employees to recognize that and

★ Stop bringing you questions

★ Shut down their creative, innovative brains

★ Become less enthusiastic about work (and possibly less productive too)

★ Leave you for a workplace where their questions are encouraged

If you are more like Manager B, you may also be highly productive. But you tend to respond eagerly and openly to your employees' questions, and you are a *question-friendly manager.* You are curious. You are used to thinking "What if that worked?" or "Why not see if we could change that policy?" or "How could this idea make us more productive?" You spend time brainstorming with your employees, and you collaborate with them to find answers to their questions.

Think about the people who first asked about these policies:

★ Job sharing

★ Flextime

★ Working remotely

★ Casual dress

★ Self-managed teams

★ Childcare centers

★ Employee ownership plans

★ Maternity/paternity leaves

These are just a few of the workplace innovations that many employees now take for granted. How would any of these ideas have been welcomed in your organization 10 years ago? How about today? If they are against the rules in your workplace, question the people who could change them.

A group of highly valued engineers from India had what some people heard as a couple of strange requests. They asked their manager to ask the senior engineering manager

- *To put carpet in their work area so they could take their shoes off and line them up against the wall, according to their custom*

- *To install a small kitchen so their wives could come in to cook their preferred Indian cuisine*

There was no precedent for this request, and the policy manual certainly didn't support it. The senior engineering manager considered the cost ($5,000) and the gain (a very happy team) and said yes. He said it was the best $5,000 he's ever spent to motivate and retain a talented work group.

This team's manager had the courage to forward their request. And the senior manager had the foresight to listen, as well as the courage to act. Are you like these managers?

Please Hold Your Questions until the End

How many times have you heard a speaker say, "Please hold your questions until the end"? Usually there is no time for questions or the speaker didn't really want questions. If you are a question-friendly manager, you welcome employee questions and innovative thoughts at any time, in any amount, and on any topic.

A question not asked is a door not opened.

—Marilee Adams, author of
Change Your Questions, Change Your Life

Imagine the talent that is lost (often to the competitor) because no one took the time to listen to the challenging questions of innovative people.

> ### ALAS
>
> *He was always too busy, and we knew we shouldn't bother him with questions or new ideas about our processes. He liked to work by the book, and he wanted us to follow the rules and just get it done. The sad thing was, our team came up with a better, faster way to turn out a superior product. We knew that if they were ever given a chance, our ideas could make money for the company. We kept our mouths shut and just kept working. I left the company and found a more innovative place to work.*
>
> —Supervisor, manufacturing team

An executive in China said that questioning is harder to do there, given the traditional education system that emphasizes knowing facts and answers. She said that you need to consider how to question safely, without causing political repercussions.

If you manage in an environment where questioning the rules is foreign and even risky, find mentors who can help you gently shift mindsets and practices that have prevented rule questioning in the past. Your employees will thank you for trying!

Too Much of a Good Thing: Rules, Guidelines, Policies, Procedures

Rules and policies are necessary to some degree, especially to effectively operate large, complex organizations. But the rules often take on a life of their own. They multiply, they live in huge manuals, and they begin to stifle productivity and creativity. One team jokingly called themselves a "ship of rules."

> Serena: *Did you know that this approval form to spend $30 came back to me after three weeks in the organization with 15 signatures, including the CFO's?*
>
> Boss: *Why on Earth would it take all of that ridiculous time and effort?*
>
> Serena: *It's the rule.*
>
> Boss: *Let's see what we can do to break that one!*

> *A Seattle hospital pulled all its employees into a large meeting room to examine the way they were doing the work. They had a mock patient enter their system. She and her paperwork moved around the room and met with people representing admissions, diagnosis, referral, and treatment. Every stop represented the accepted rule and step for either the patient or her paperwork. The exercise revealed (to the horror of everyone) that one patient and her paperwork had made 50 stops through a bureaucratic maze before she began treatment.*

Overgrown rules sometimes need questioning. If your talented employees get bogged down in them, they will spend too much time navigating the bureaucracy, not to mention filling out paperwork. They will spend too little time innovating and creating new solutions, services, or products. They will also look for an opportunity to work elsewhere, in a freer workplace with fewer rules and restrictions.

> *In Russia there is a saying: rules are meant to be gotten around (not broken). This is challenging for those of us involved in making the rules. However, I have noticed that there is nothing quite so deflating as telling someone what the policy says.*
> —Manager, PepsiCo, Russia

→ TRY THIS

★ Encourage your employees' questions. Ask them to ask you the questions that matter to them. Tell them that any time is a good time to ask.

★ Support your employees' attempts to reduce the number of rules in your organization. Suggest they form a *silly rules committee* to stamp out rules that are—you got it—silly.

★ Hold regular rule-busting meetings just to look at rules, systems, and procedures that no longer work. Put different employees in charge of each meeting. Fight for the reexamination of a rule you *know* needs to go!

Leadership is not as much about knowing the right answers as it is about asking the right questions. Leaders who lead with questions will often be 10 times more effective than leaders who only lead by telling.
—Bob Tiede, author of *Great Leaders Ask Questions*

Are You Boxed In?

You have no doubt been asked (probably more than once) to think "outside the box." How ironic that most managers feel like the box has been handed to them (often by their bosses) and that they are supposed to think and act inside it. The box typically feels fairly rigid, as if it were made of concrete walls—the rules. But with a shift in thinking, your box can be composed of different materials, each with unique properties. A video titled *Joshua in a Box* provides the example illustrated in figure 17.1.[1]

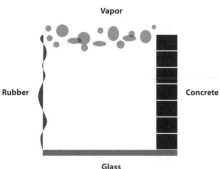

Figure 17.1. The four walls

The box has walls made of four materials:

★ **Concrete.** This wall represents rules that are truly rigid. It cannot be broken, pushed, bent, or shattered. *"You must have a medical degree to practice medicine in this hospital."*

★ **Glass.** This wall is strong and sturdy, but if you hit it just the right way with just the right instrument at the right time, it will break. It represents the rules that may seem unbreakable but actually can be broken. *"A woman will never be CEO of a major corporation."*

★ **Rubber.** This wall is thick and strong, but it has some give to it if you are willing to push hard. It represents rules that might be pliable. *"We all put in a 40-hour week, from eight to five, five days a week."*

★ **Vapor.** This wall is made up of our beliefs, assumptions, and perceptions about the rules. *"Cars will never park themselves."*

If you examine the rules you operate by, you will find that few of them are truly concrete. They just feel that way. The most formidable aspect of the box is often the vapor wall. Your beliefs and assumptions—or the company's—often prevent you from questioning the rules. They may also keep you from hearing your employees' questions.

We all had a great test of rule questioning in the early months of the coronavirus pandemic, when suddenly established ways of doing business had to be redesigned in a hurry. Leaders at all levels quickly sensed that rule questioning had become the new norm and scrambled to find ways to get work done while protecting themselves and their employees from a deadly virus. As thousands of workers adapted quickly to Zoom meetings from home, the beliefs and assumptions about on-site versus remote working came under scrutiny.

As you self-reflect, consider how the vapor wall impacts how you include those who are different from you. What do you assume they can or can't do?

Human Potential Project is an organization that specializes in experiential learning and high-performance team building for managers. One exercise in a weeklong training session is to climb a 30-foot pole and leap off the top to catch a trapeze (supported by safety lines, of course). One group included a paraplegic manager in a wheelchair who wanted very much to take part in all the activities. Many in the group had a vapor wall of beliefs and assumptions that said he could not be part of the pole exercise. But he insisted, the trainers huddled, and between them they found a solution. He climbed the pole, using the strength of his arms and the support of safety lines, while his team shouted from below. When he reached the top, he cried—and so did we.

—Former trainer, Human Potential Project

That manager and the trainers who worked with him found a way around the vapor. When the event was over, the manager said, "I will forever be willing to test assumptions (mine and others') and find work-arounds to the barriers life presents."

→ TRY THIS

★ The next time your employees question you about the rules (about their jobs, the organization, or the work at hand), stop before you say, "It can't be done."

★ Check to see which wall is holding you (and others) in the box.

★ Unless it is truly the concrete wall, work with your employees to bend or break the rules. Test the vapor wall and the beliefs that box you in. Evaluate new ideas fairly before you discard them.

A manager in a large landscaping company took a look at the rules (mostly vapor) that had him boxed in. His entire team is made up of Gen Ys, and he is a boomer. He realized that operating by the rules of his generation was hindering his ability to engage and retain younger talent. He decided to let his team do two things that seemed outrageous to him but absolutely normal to them. He said they could paint the office any color (or colors) they wanted, and they could listen to their music while they worked. The team was ecstatic. They painted the office in modern, bright colors, happily donned their earbuds, and went to work! Productivity and commitment soared. The manager is thrilled he reconsidered the "rules."

Question Yourself Too

Not only do you need to be able to ask good questions of others, but the best managers we know also are able to ask good questions of themselves. They are able to step back and question actions they have taken and even consider actions they haven't taken. Their continual self-examination catches on with their employees. Here are some questions you might try, adapted with permission from Marilee Adams's book *Change Your Questions, Change Your Life*:[2]

★ What happened?

★ What's useful about this?

★ What do I want?

★ What can I learn?

★ What is the other person thinking, feeling, needing, and wanting?

★ How can this be a win-win?

★ What's possible?

★ What are my choices?

★ What is best to do now?

★ How inclusive am I? How could I be even more inclusive?

If You Manage Managers

Are the managers you manage bound by the rules? By your rules? If they are, their teams may be less creative and productive than they could be. Check out how you're modeling effective rule bending. Then expect your managers to model and encourage questioning the rules, and support their efforts. Which rules no longer make sense? Invite your managers to have a "silly rules" chat at the next staff meeting.

BOTTOM LINE

How long has it been since you questioned the rules? And how much do you encourage questioning? Allow your employees to ask about the way work gets done and about the rules that hinder their productivity and satisfaction. Really listen, support their questioning, and bend or break the rules to help them get what they need. You will greatly increase the odds of keeping your talent.

Q

CHAPTER EIGHTEEN

Reward

PROVIDE RECOGNITION

Ponder this: Which matters more, praise or pay?

So this is the chapter about money, right? Isn't money a major motivator to stay?

Decades of research and common sense tell you to pay fairly or your best people might leave. Benchmark similar organizations in your industry, and find out what the pay scales, bonuses, and perks look like. If you find that your compensation system is not competitive with that of similar companies, be concerned. Take your findings to your boss or to the compensation expert in your company and try to get things changed.

Pay fairly and *pay competitively. But don't stop there.* The research that suggests you need to pay fairly to keep your people also says that money alone won't keep them on your team. *Money is not the major motivator.* Challenge, growth opportunities, flexibility, great coworkers, meaningful work, a boss who values them, and recognition (often in nonmonetary forms) are examples of things that matter more to most of your people. When those are missing, talented people walk.

> *The deepest principle of human nature is the craving to be appreciated.*
>
> —William James

Multiple studies around the globe tell us that a majority of people leave their jobs because they don't feel appreciated. What about your employees? Ask them how they are recognized and appreciated. If they immediately respond with "You notice my contributions" or "You thank me all the time," then you're doing great. If they stare blankly at you and then finally say, "Do you mean my paycheck?" you might have some work to do in the rewards department. Stay tuned.

A Word about Perks

What exactly is a perk? It's short for perquisite and is also known as a privilege, a gratuity, a bonus. Do perks work to engage and retain talent?

> *At my company you can do your laundry; drop off your dry cleaning; get an oil change, then have your car washed; work out in the gym; attend subsidized exercise classes; get a massage; study Mandarin, Japanese, and French; and ask a concierge to arrange dinner reservations. How about in your company?*
> —Research and development manager, Silicon Valley company

In the last 20 years, we've seen the proliferation of everything from volleyball courts to BMW giveaways to concierge services in an attempt to improve work life and to retain talent. While these perks may have worked to recruit some people, and they are often received happily by the workforce, no evidence exists that they will help you hang on to your stars. If your highly marketable employees are bored, don't like the boss, or see no career future with you, a massage won't keep them.

When a Reward Backfires

ALAS

I was so excited. I got an email from the human resources manager saying, "Congratulations, you have been nominated for an accomplishment award. If your supervisor hasn't told you yet, you will be honored at our next department-wide staff meeting" (about 300 people). I quickly wrote back a thank-you and waited for my supervisor to say something. Then my colleague popped up and said she got the same email. While I was happy for her, she had been in our unit for only a few weeks. Then I learned that our entire unit was nominated—all 10 of us plus 7 others who were no longer in our section! A month went by and there was another congratulation *from the head of the department. Nothing from my supervisor. Another month went by and it was time for the staff meeting. There we were (all 17) in front of the department of 300, taking pictures and trying to smile. The next day we learned from HR that the award included money—hooray! But the total dollars would be split among all of us! Still no hint, conversation, or high-five from my supervisor. When it was all said and done, I did get $35.*

—Frontline worker for manufacturing firm

This is a classic backfire story that illustrates the difference between intent and impact. The intention was to reward *everyone*. The impact was that no one felt truly rewarded.

Culture-Conscious Rewarding

As with every chapter in this book, we've focused again on learning about your talented employees' preferences to best engage and retain them. Depending on the size and function of your organization, you might also need to identify recognition preferences on a much larger (even global) scale.

One of my clients recently announced the restructuring of their global rewards program. In the past, when they've given a $100 reward (US dollars) for a certain level of achievement in the US, they've simply converted the dollars into Chinese currency for a Chinese employee who achieved at a comparable level. But the equivalent of $100 US is a much bigger reward in China. So now they're evening out the value of their rewards around the world to make the program more fair.

—Communications consultant in Los Angeles

Is your organization growing? Becoming more multinational or multicultural? If so, you might need to modify your recognition strategies to accommodate the growing diversity. For example, in Australia and Mexico, team recognition seems to be important, while in Germany, China, India, and Japan, many employees prefer individual recognition.[1] You'll do well to learn about these and other cultural preferences as you design a recognition system with a *long* reach.

Think about how you will do the following:

★ Recognize global similarities and local nuances

★ Keep your recognition efforts fair and consistent across organizational boundaries, functions, and cultures

★ Adapt recognition methods to employees' local and cultural preferences

★ Model and encourage global salutes to teammates abroad who do great work

And, most importantly, remember to *ask* all employees what kinds of rewards they most value.

Reward Rules

Rule #1: Rewards Need to Match Your Employees' Needs and Wants

How would you like to be recognized? We asked dozens of people this question. Some of what we heard is listed below. Notice that the answers vary greatly and are informed by upbringing, culture, work experience, personality, and more.

→ TRY THIS

Check which forms of recognition you might appreciate. Also note which ones might not matter to you. All of these are requests employees have made to their managers.

☐ An award, preferably given in front of my peers

☐ A plaque to hang on my wall

☐ A thank-you, in writing, from my boss

☐ A note to my boss's boss about my excellent performance

☐ Frequent pats on the back

☐ Implementation by my boss of one of my ideas

☐ A chance to be on a really exciting, cutting-edge project

☐ A day off

☐ Words of praise in front of my family

☐ A chance to go to lunch with senior management

☐ An opportunity to work with people from other parts of the company

☐ A chance to be on one of the important steering committees

☐ A change in my title

☐ Some flexibility in my schedule

☐ More freedom or autonomy

☐ A seminar or training class

Many managers wrongly assume that everyone likes or wants the same types of rewards and recognition.

I will never forget the thrill of receiving an Excellence Award at the annual company conference. Seven hundred of my peers were there. My name was called and written in huge letters across a massive screen. As I walked forward, it truly felt like an Academy Award moment—almost surreal. There was a cash prize that accompanied a beautiful glass trophy inscribed with my name. I had my picture taken with senior management.

The cash was spent within weeks. But the trophy still sits on my desk, and the memory of that amazing moment of recognition will last a lifetime. I have never felt more appreciated or rewarded.
                                    —Vice president, major consulting firm

While this person felt fully rewarded by being in the spotlight at the conference, someone else might have been embarrassed. An audience participant in Asia said that in her culture, "The nail that sticks out gets hammered down. It's often awkward for individuals to receive public recognition for their excellence. They view it as just doing their duty."

Rule #2: If an Employee Expects It, It May No Longer Be Viewed as a Reward

ALAS

Every year I received a bonus, some stock options, and a raise. I was hitting all the targets and doing a good job. It's funny how I left every one of those annual reviews feeling empty. The reward I wanted most was positive feedback from my boss. I wanted him to say that he really appreciated me and my contributions to the business. I really never felt recognized. That was a primary reason I left the company for another job.
                                    —Manager, global automobile manufacturer

You may think that the annual incentive bonus is ample reward for work well done. Your employee may see it differently. Many employees now expect bonuses, company cars, cell phones, financial planning services, and great healthcare plans as part of the package. Those are no longer useful as special reward or recognition tools.

Ask your employees what kind of recognition or reward they most appreciate. Note: In some cultures and some companies, the answer could be "Whatever you want to give is fine." Be patient. Ask "what else?" a few more times and you'll learn how to reward your treasured employee.

The Universal Reward

Don't you just love the words in figure 18.1? Think about how you felt the last time someone thanked you. If it feels so good to receive thanks, why would we so often fail to give it?

Figure 18.1. Many ways to say thanks

Many otherwise able managers act as if compliments come out of their bank accounts.

—Warren Bennis, author/consultant

Check your files. Somewhere in there is a letter from a boss thanking you for a job well done, right? You've cleaned out all the others over the years, but this letter of praise remains. Why is that? Praise works for everyone. There's really no such thing as too much praise (as long as it's sincere). Regardless of individual differences, virtually all employees want to hear what great work they have done. And they are happy to hear it again and again.

Compensation is a right; recognition is a gift.

—Rosabeth Moss Kanter, professor, Harvard Business School

→ TRY THIS

We suggest praising your employees in the following ways, taking individual preferences into account:

★ **Privately.** Go to your employee's office to give a personal thank-you and praise. (*Verbal* thank-yous are critical.)

★ **Publicly.** Praise an employee in the presence of others (peers, family members, your boss). One team adds "shameless bragging" as a short agenda item in all staff meetings.

★ **Spontaneously.** Catch people doing something right and thank them then and there. (Thank you, Ken Blanchard, author of *The One Minute Manager.*) Leave voice or email recognition messages. It takes less than one minute.

★ **Specifically.** Praise people for specific (rather than generic) accomplishments or efforts. See "Sentence Starters for Engaging Your Best Employees," coming up.

★ **In writing.** Send a card, letter, memo, or email. Possibly send a copy to team members or higher-level management. Don't forget—*written* thank-yous are a coveted workplace incentive.

A nurse had worked at her hospital for five years, giving more than the job required. However, she had not received much positive feedback along the way. Recently she got a thank-you note in the mail from her manager, telling her how much he appreciated the hard work and extra efforts. That card meant so much to her that she is now carrying it around in her purse. She said the thank-you—knowing that her manager appreciates her efforts— "makes all the hard work worthwhile."

R

Sentence Starters for Engaging Your Best Employees

Silent gratitude isn't of much use to anyone.
—Gladys Bronwyn Stern

Praise can help you engage and retain your good people, especially if it is specific. Here are some openers you might use. Put them in the notes app on your cell phone and send yourself a calendar reminder to try one or more of them:

★ "You really made a difference by . . ."

★ "I'm impressed with . . ."

★ "You got my attention with . . ."

★ "You're doing top quality work on . . ."

★ "You're right on the mark with . . ."

★ "One of the things I enjoy most about you is . . ."

★ "You can be proud of yourself for . . ."

★ "We couldn't have done it without your . . ."

★ "What an effective way to . . ."

★ "You've made my day because of . . ."

You can also use these sentence starters with your colleagues—or spouse.

Get Creative

As you struggle to think of other ways to reward and recognize your employees, try this: think about yourself. What could your boss do that would really demonstrate how much he or she values you (besides giving you a raise or praise)? Remembering individual differences, you can use your own list to think about how to reward your employees. Here are a few hints that will get you started.

Time

Give an outstanding employee the afternoon off. Allow another to sleep late. Thank a whole team by giving them a day off. Let them decide when to use their gift of time.

Toys

What toys might the team want? A cappuccino machine? A dart board or foosball table in the lounge? Tickets to a movie?

Trophies and Trinkets

What small memento or trophy would be meaningful? It could be a customized plaque, a coffee cup inscribed with a personal thank-you note, or a refrigerator magnet with the perfect message. Often these forms of recognition bring bragging rights and give people a chance to say, "I was recognized because . . ."

Simple observation suggests that most of us are trinket freaks—if they represent a genuine thanks for a genuine assist.
—Tom Peters, author and management consultant

Fun

Would your employees like to take an outing on company time? Leave work early to play ball or to take a hike together? Go to a movie? Have a spontaneous pizza party in the office some afternoon?

Freedom

What kind of freedom might they want? Flextime? Freedom to work from home, to dress casually, to change the way they do some of the work? Freedom to work without supervision? Freedom to manage a budget?

Food

Some of the most popular low-cost rewards are food. One manager we know asks all new hires what their favorite candy is and then delivers that candy to them on their six-month anniversary. (Bev loves Chuckles; Sharon loves peanut M&M's.) And people love gift certificates for dinner at a great restaurant. (Dinner for two is wonderful—dinner for the family is fantastic.)

Small Money

A reward can be a small sum ($50–$100) to put toward whatever the rewarded employee wants. This discretionary, on-the-spot cash award is sometimes more deeply appreciated than you might guess.

R

One internal marketing group in a medium-sized manufacturing company decided to reward people they worked with each month. They set aside $1,200 so that they could present a $100 gift certificate to a person from another department who had helped them in some way and was appreciated. The entire marketing team selected the recipient, and each month one person surprised the recipient by presenting the gift at an unexpected time. Everyone loved the idea. The marketing department enjoyed the process, and it was "small money."

Big Money

Compete on culture, not on money. There will always be a higher bidder. Make your workplace so desirable that your talent cannot be enticed away by dollars.

Money might help you get talented people in your door, but it will seldom keep them. Yet it may be exactly what some people want. Find out which of your talented employees is truly motivated by money. See what you can do for them. Would a bonus for exceeding goals and expectations help? How about a larger raise than expected? Think about where you can stretch your budget to reward with money when it is warranted and *desired*. Remember, it will usually cost you more to replace stars than to meet their salary requests.

If you think your hands are tied because more dollars aren't available, try this: tell the truth. Then ask what else your employee might want. You will discover at least one thing your talented employee wants that you can give. The key is that you let employees know how much you value them and their contributions.

People are the only asset an organization has that can appreciate over time . . . if we truly appreciate them.
—Anonymous

If You Manage Managers

Notice how the managers you manage are rewarding their talent. Ask them their favorite ways of recognizing all-out effort and work well done. If they have to search for an answer, it's time to give them some ideas about this crucial aspect of excellent leadership. Dedicate a staff meeting to discuss this topic and create a menu of rewards. How are you modeling this important behavior? What are your managers learning from you?

BOTTOM LINE

Over and over, research tells us that money is not the major key to engaging and keeping good people. We double-checked this research with our own, and it proves true. When employees across the globe answer the question "What keeps you?" few have dollars in their top three reasons. People want recognition for work well done. Assess your pay scale to be sure it's fair. Then praise your good people. Find creative ways to show your appreciation, and you will increase the odds of keeping them.

R

CHAPTER NINETEEN

Space

GIVE IT

Ponder this: How many of your employees feel like they're on a short leash?

Give me some space! Anyone who has raised a teenager or remembers being one knows that phrase. We hear it when people feel fenced in, overcontrolled, or frustrated by their lack of power over their own situation. Dilbert, the cartoon spokesperson for office workers, constantly profiles managers as control freaks who give their employees little or no space, either physically (cubicles) or figuratively (space to control one's own day-to-day existence).

Think about the last boss you had who dictated your every move, held stringently to the policy manual, or was never open to new ways of doing anything. How long did you stay in that job? (We hope you are not there now.) That boss didn't understand inner space or outer space. Employees will leave if they don't have enough of both.

Inner and Outer Space

By *inner space*, we mean the mental and emotional space your employees want and need to feel like creative, productive members of the team. It includes space to

★   Be self-directed

★   Manage their own time

★   Work and think in new ways

As a manager, you can give your talented employees the inner space they want and increase the odds that they will stay on your team. (It usually costs you nothing.)

Outer space refers to the physical world and primarily to employees' work environment. It includes space to

★ Design their own work area

★ Work from different places

★ Take a break

★ Dress as they wish

Managing your employees' outer space requests might require some boundary-pushing behaviors for you, especially if your organization has never done it that way. Before we tell you what some other managers are doing to give more space, take this short quiz to determine your own space-giving tendencies.

→ TRY THIS

Read these scenarios, imagining that you're this team's boss and that they are making these diverse requests of you. When would you say, "Sure," "No way," or "Let me see what I can do"?

1. I want to come in half an hour earlier and leave half an hour earlier three days a week.

2. I want to get this task done in a brand-new way, not as you have seen it done before.

3. I want to complete the first five steps of this project before you review it.

4. I want to try a novel and new approach to increase sales.

5. Instead of taking that class you recommended, I found a mentor to teach me that skill.

6. I just took some great vacation photos and want to put them on my office/cubicle walls.

7. I want to work from home two days a week.

8. I plan to work on Saturdays for a few weeks to finish a project on time. I want to bring my well-trained dog to work with me on those days.

9. I want to wear casual clothes to work, rather than a business suit.

10. I know we've always done these projects solo, but I want to put together a team this time because I believe we will do the job better and more quickly.

11. I want six weeks off work (without pay) to begin building my own home (or to travel, study, care for my parent).

12. I want to bring my baby to work occasionally.

To which requests did you say, "No way"? Are you sure there isn't a way?

In some organizations, every one of these requests would receive a positive response. But the opposite is true in far too many. Would you be surprised to know that those organizations are not on anyone's preferred employer list and that they are having greater difficulty recruiting and retaining their employees? We believe that no matter how well these organizations pay, they will ultimately lose their talented people, simply because they do not give them *space*.

Give Outer Space

Space to Work from Different Places at Different Times

President Barack Obama, speaking at a workplace forum, said, "Work is what you do, not where you do it." For many managers today, an important part of the job entails creating a workplace that encourages deep connections among colleagues, whether they sit side by side or across the globe from each other.

Does your organization support flexible work arrangements? Do you? A 2019 survey found 61 percent of global companies allow their staff to have some sort of remote working opportunity.[1] Many managers who've tried it say that remote workers tend to work longer hours because they feel telecommuting is a privilege and they want to make sure they don't lose it. Productivity and morale go up, while turnover and real estate costs go down.

Remote working instantly became the norm for thousands of employees and leaders at all levels when the global pandemic began. Thousands of workers and their managers found it worked well for them and decided to continue the practice. Some say that remote working is here to stay, especially as new and better technology emerges.

We'll no doubt continue to study and debate the pros and cons of that major shift for years to come.

> *Job performance of employees working at least partially from home is clearly increased. Employees working in company offices are interrupted from their work on average, every 11 minutes— and then need 8 minutes to regain full concentration.*
>
> —Hartmut Schulze, professor, University of
> Applied Sciences and Arts, Switzerland

But what if your organization does not allow flexible work arrangements?

> *One of my top employees asked me if she could work from home two days a week, and my immediate response was no. A month later she handed in her resignation and said she had found a job where she could telecommute. I could not afford to lose her, so I went to my boss and asked if we might bend the rules on a trial basis, offer her telecommuting two days a week, and see how productive she was. She stayed with us, increased her actual productivity by 10 percent, and is a grateful, loyal employee. Since then we have loosened our policy substantially and consider telecommuting on a case-by-case basis for any employee who requests it.*
>
> —Accounting manager, city government in Switzerland

This manager not only bent the rules but also realized the importance of space.

Telecommuting is not an option for jobs that simply must be performed at the work site. (Consider a nurse on duty, the landscaper at your home, a factory worker on the line.) If the work site is the only place your employees can perform their jobs, think about other ways that you can give them space.

Sometimes the organization has no rule against working from another place, but the manager says no anyway. If you are one of those managers, ask yourself why. Is it a lack of trust in your employees? Is it concern that they will goof off or not be productive without your ever-vigilant eye? If so, consider managing based on results. Be clear about your expectations: what do you want them to produce or create?

By when? Consider letting your employees get those results from whatever location they wish.

Space to Take a Break

Seldom do we find managers who value their employees enough to allow them the space to take a real break from work. Yet in many countries and in certain fields (such as college teaching), sabbaticals are actually encouraged. Employers support valuable employees in their decisions to travel, learn something new, or simply go to the mountains and meditate. The next time your talented employee asks you for a break, get creative (with the employee) about finding a way to make it happen. Your employee will feel supported, and the odds of your retaining that talent will go up.

S

A talented young engineer in a large aerospace firm asked his boss for six weeks off work (without pay) to begin building his house. His boss said okay, even though the engineer's absence would certainly be a hardship. After the six weeks, the engineer asked for an additional four weeks, as he hadn't done as much as he had hoped on his house. The boss pondered the request, thought about how valued this employee was, ran the request up to the division engineer, and came back with the okay. The engineer remained a loyal, committed employee for another 24 years. He later became a member of the senior management team and helped lead his company to tremendous success. When asked what he would have done had his request been turned down, he said he would have quit the job and found a new one after completing his project.

Space to Dress How One Wishes

We have all read about the high-tech environment in which people with creative, brilliant minds dress in all kinds of unique outfits. Some wonder if it is appropriate or professional or conducive to productivity. The results seem to speak for themselves. Just take a look at successful companies where there are *no dress codes* in many departments. How productive have they been over the years? Managers in those environments say that their employees often work long hours (sometimes 70-hour weeks) by their own choosing as they strive to complete a project or get a new product out the door. Allowing them to dress as they wish seems a small concession, considering the commitment and high productivity.

I don't feel I need to dress up to meet an equation.

—Mathematician

Think about where you can offer flexibility in dress. Is it Friday-casual day? Summer attire? Different dress codes for those who never see a customer? Challenge the rules a bit. Are they reasonable? If business wear is truly necessary, then you will want to support the rule—but think about the requirements realistically and with a creative eye. It is truly amazing how favorably many employees view a flexible dress code.

Creating an inclusive culture requires taking differences into account. That includes differences in attire. Check your biases and assumptions about what is proper dress. Workplace attire could easily be as diverse and unique as the talented people on your team.

Space to Design One's Space

Should all work areas in your organization look alike? Anyone who has studied personality differences knows that one way we express our uniqueness is in our surroundings. Our homes, our offices, and our cubicles will reflect our style if we have the freedom.

Many organizations today hire interior decorating firms that design beautiful, perfect work areas. In some of those workplaces, the decorating rules are explicit, and there is no room for personalization. What about your organization? If the rules allow for some flexibility, then you as a manager have room to allow space for your employees. Let them bring in their favorite pictures and organize their desks the way they wish. Do not demand that everyone have a workspace like yours.

Workers' cubicles could be their castles—with a little help. One manager gave his employees a small decorating stipend for personalizing their workplaces. They were thrilled and have done some very creative things to make their cubes their castles. With a little bigger budget, workers have opted for changes like these to their workspaces:

★ Cubicle walls that hold oxygen-giving plant life, complete with built-in irrigation

★ Adjustable desks to accommodate needs

★ Shorter walls and privacy shields to allow for more or less interaction

★ Noise-canceling headphones to facilitate concentration

★ Foldout chairs to welcome guests to a small space

Several Singapore managers helped design a new office layout where their employees' workstations overlooked the harbor, while the managers occupied the *view-free* middle of the space. How amazing is that?

Give Inner Space

Space to Be Self-Directed—to Work and Think in One's Own Unique Ways

Giving inner space requires that managers let go and trust their talented employees to manage and continuously improve their work.

Leaders at a large retail store know a lot about giving employees space and empowering them to make decisions and manage their own work. In fact, managers credit their corporate culture for one of the highest retention rates in the retail industry. The primary rule, stated in the employee handbook, is this: use your good judgment at all times.

Space-friendly managers have

★ Pushed for nap rooms for employees who need a midmorning or afternoon snooze to reenergize

★ Said "sure" to their younger employees who wanted to work while listening to their music

★ Allowed an employee to work on his laptop on the lawn (where he could think)

→ TRY THIS

★ Let your employees manage more aspects of their own work, without direct supervision.

★ Trust them to get it right and then assist when they need your help.

★ Allow them to try new ways of accomplishing their tasks, even if "it's never been done that way before."

You probably have plenty of leeway as a manager to give inner space to your employees, and the payoff is tremendous. If you cannot offer telecommuting or casual dress codes, you can offer the power to manage the way they do their day-to-day work.

Space to Manage One's Own Time

All the research points to the fact that emerging workers (of any age) want flexibility in work schedules. So what are organizations doing in response to these wants?

A large medical center found the job market for medical professionals such as nurses and pharmacists was, in part, driving flexible scheduling. Offering schedules to fit various lifestyles and needs made the organization more competitive. For example, one emergency room nurse chose to work a "power weekend," which has her on duty for 12 hours on Saturday and Sunday, with time off during the week to pick up her grandchildren at school and attend their sporting events.

—Director, human resources

What if yours isn't one of these flex-friendly employers? This may be another area where you say, "I have no control. Our organization has strict policies about work hours and how and where they are spent." If that is true, then you will want to consider other ways of offering space to your employees. However, we encourage you to see where there *might* be some flexibility to offer your employees space to manage their work time according to their own unique needs.

One supervisor we know allowed workers to arrive one hour before their shifts began and leave one hour earlier or vice versa. He realized that this flexibility could substantially reduce driving time during rush hours, making a huge difference in his employees' stress.

And consider the B-Society, a group in Denmark lobbying for businesses to be flexible and accommodate people who just can't get going before 10 or 11 in the morning. Accommodating the B-Society late-sleepers has gained worldwide popularity. Can you find a way to harness the energy of your talent when they're at their best?

What about Fairness?

Our readers have asked us about fairness: "How do I give one employee time off on Friday afternoon and not give it to everyone?" Being fair does not mean treating everyone identically.

Do you have more than one child? If so, do you give them all identical holiday gifts? Probably not.

The answer is mass customization (sounds like an oxymoron, doesn't it?), and it offers a new kind of institutional fairness. The workforce is more differentiated, and one policy simply does not fit all. (Who said management was easy?) Listen to your talented employees' requests, and brainstorm with them to create innovative solutions that are *fair*, both to them and to their talented teammates.

Of course, there's a catch. Sure, you can take Friday off to train for the Ironman Triathlon or to attend your kid's soccer match. Just make sure you do your job—and figure out how to do it better than anyone else. With freedom and flexibility come responsibility and accountability—lots of it.

—Paula Lawlor, MediHealth Outsourcing

If You Manage Managers

Ask the managers you manage to take the space quiz on page 172. Invite them to share their findings. To which requests did they say, "No way"? Then have a discussion. Help them consider multiple ways of giving space in your department, given the culture and the work people do. Request that they, like you, ask "what if?" before saying no when a talented employee makes an unusual request.

BOTTOM LINE

Allowing job sharing, flextime, telecommuting, or working on the lawn on a laptop is not pampering. These options are ways to meet your business goals and retain talent. That means listening to what people want, going to bat for their needs, and ultimately giving them options and opportunities to do things differently. Truly listen to the diverse requests your employees bring you. Ask them to provide ideas for how this change might work—for you, the team, and the organization. Make an honest attempt to win flexibility and improved work conditions for your people.

CHAPTER TWENTY

Truth
TELL IT

Ponder this: How many of your employees really know where they stand?

Our studies show that employees yearn for straight talk. They want to *hear* the truth about their performance and the organization. They want to *tell you* the truth about your performance. When the truth is missing, people may feel demoralized, less confident, and ultimately less loyal. Of course you know where that might lead—right out your door and through the competition's. Tell the truth if you want to engage and keep your good people.

A New View of Truth Telling

The secret of truth telling is to view it as a *gift*. If you believe that giving truthful, balanced feedback to people will help them be more effective in their careers and perhaps in life, then you will be more inclined to give (and get) feedback.

> *After getting feedback, a UK sales manager with a good sense of humor said, "Thanks . . . send socks next time."*

Have you ever taken music, dance, or karate lessons or had a soccer, rugby, or golf coach? Think back to that time and recall one of your lessons.

Did your coach demonstrate a better way to grip the club? Did your teacher help you develop better rhythm? Weren't they constantly helping you fine-tune your approach? The feedback was probably balanced between *praise*—"That was great. Play it again just like that!"—and *correction*—"This time kick the ball more like this." Their gift was honest feedback, from someone willing to tell you there was still room for improvement and committed to helping you get there.

Your employees expect and need the same kind of coaching from you today.

Trust Is the Backdrop

Trust is the backdrop for any authentic, important conversation.[1] That's true for stay interviews and certainly for feedback meetings with your talented people. They need to trust that you genuinely care about them, want to learn more about them, and have their backs.

What if you don't believe that trust exists yet? Should you avoid giving frequent honest developmental feedback to your talented people? No. It's paradoxical. It's true that giving helpful feedback is easier and more successful when you're trusted—and that giving helpful feedback *builds* trust. Go figure.

In addition, seeking feedback from your team demonstrates your humility and shows you value their input. It is, in fact, a trust generator.

Tell Them the Truth about Their Work

Think about the people who work with you or report to you. Consider their relative strengths and weaknesses, their blind spots, their overused strengths, and the flaws that may stall them. Have you been honest and direct about your perceptions with these people?

> *I wish I could have a dollar for the number of occasions I've had to untangle a situation where at the outset if there had been a clear, thoughtful expression of truth, there would be no mess!*
> —Matt Hawkins, former leadership development facilitator,
> Tandem Ministries, New Zealand

When and how did you give them your input? Even the best bosses might honestly confess that they have trouble giving people direct feedback, especially about possible flaws or areas where employees need improvement. Most of us were not trained to give negative news. So we don't.

Managers say they hesitate to give critical feedback because they

★   Want to be liked

★ Are afraid of hurting feelings or demoralizing employees—
  even prompting them to quit

★ Are concerned about appearing arrogant or abrasive

★ Are uncomfortable giving bad news or find it easier to give
  only positive news

★ Are not sure they're 100 percent right

★ Worry about a defensive reaction

★ Work in a polite organization where critical feedback isn't given

★ Don't like to judge other people

What's your excuse?

ALAS

I honestly thought I was doing a great job. I had been promoted several times, had had positive performance reviews, and had received a bonus every year. The next thing I knew, I was passed over for a big promotion, shoved in a corner, and ignored. When the downsizing happened, I was laid off. Only then did I hear that there had been some problems with my management style through the years.

—Unemployed middle manager

Ask Them for Their View

Consider asking your employees to provide their own points of view first. What is their view of the past quarter? What areas of their performance do they feel best about? What successes have they had? Probe for the specific skills they used.

Also ask what they might do to be even more effective. Where do they most need to grow? Ask them about a recent project that they might do differently if they had the chance. Ask what they learned from the experience. Most employees know the answers to these questions, especially if they're fortunate enough to have had truth-telling managers.

Share your own stories about feedback received and lessons learned.

T

The Truth Hurts—or Does It?

When employees in most organizations are asked what they would like more of from their managers, their first response is usually *feedback*. People want to know where they stand—they want to know if your perception of their performance is the same as their own.

Years of research confirms that the absence of honest feedback derails leaders at all levels. Sometimes that means people lose their jobs, but more often it means they fail to fulfill their promise.

Even the high-potentials in your organization need honest, balanced feedback. Too often they hear only how wonderful, bright, and talented they are. Without feedback, these employees can come to a startling, shocking halt after several promotions, big raises, and starring roles. Why? Because no one helped them see their rough edges and the need for continual improvement. They began to believe their own press and developed major blind spots. Their confidence turned into arrogance, in part because of insufficient, inaccurate, imbalanced, or tardy feedback from key people in their lives. The truth could have saved them.

→ TRY THIS

Ask these questions of your employees:

★ If you asked three people in the organization to give you feedback on your greatest strength, what would they say? And your greatest liability?

★ What's your reputation at work? How do you know? How will you find out?

★ Whose feedback would you value? How and when will you ask for that?

Message to those I coach: Become a "feedback junkie"; ask the boss, but don't stop there. Ask colleagues, customers, direct reports, and your partner, if you dare. Ask often. Use the 1-to-10 approach [see below] to get the fine-tuning feedback you need to excel over time.

—Sharon Jordan-Evans, executive coach

The 1-to-10 Approach

Here's a surefire way to get feedback without putting someone on the spot:

> **Employee:** On a 1-to-10 scale, how did I do in that meeting?
>
> **Feedback provider:** Oh, you did great. You were a 9.5.
>
> **Employee:** Thanks so much! What would make me a 10?
>
> **Feedback provider** (*thinking*): Well, maybe you could have more eye contact with those in the back of the room. Or perhaps add a touch of humor—appropriate, of course—to your PowerPoint deck, just to hold their attention.

The result? The employee got some fine-tuning feedback that could include brand-new information or a reminder of something he already knew. His feedback provider was comfortable because she could give him a great score and still provide ideas for his continued improvement. Everyone wins.

The Velcro/Teflon Phenomenon

Remember when you got mostly positive feedback from your favorite teacher, best boss, or spouse? There was just that one thing you needed to change; there were a dozen things you were doing right. Which do you remember? You got it. You hung on to the negative and dismissed the positive. Author M. Tamra Chandler says, "When you receive negative stimuli, it sticks in your brain as if it were made of Velcro. On the other hand, when positive information arrives, it's likely to slide off as easily as a fried egg in a Teflon pan."[2]

Our neuroscientist friends can describe exactly what happens in the brain when we get negative or positive feedback. They can tell you why the negative input you received last year is still sticking like Velcro but you can't recall one positive message from that meeting. We know it's human and normal and somehow connected to our basic survival instincts.

So as you think about and prepare for giving (or receiving) honest feedback, be aware of this phenomenon. Recognize it in yourself and in others. Normalize it and gently remind yourself and your talented people to take a long look at the good news too. Then address the ways you might learn, grow, seek help, succeed, and celebrate.

T

"But I Already Gave Feedback—in December"

Many organizations require managers to give feedback only during the annual performance review. They give input to reward and reinforce employees' behaviors and performance, to justify the annual raise, or to warn them about unsatisfactory performance and possible consequences. Some managers gloss over the negatives and focus on the good news only, and others do just the opposite. In either case, the reviews don't tell the whole truth, and employees are often left frustrated by the whole process.

Consider these two points:

★ Formal performance appraisal meetings are important. If you handle it badly, your employees may feel dismissed and unimportant. Plan carefully and balance the good news (positive) with the corrective news (room for improvement).

★ Don't give feedback just once a year. To retain your key people, it is essential that you give regular, honest input about their work. This is true for everyone but especially important for younger generations who are used to and expect frequent, straightforward feedback. Their video games provide that; why shouldn't you?

ALAS

In our organization, the employee and boss both fill out the performance appraisal form once a year. The idea is to compare results and discuss the employee's performance. I spent hours completing mine, really trying to evaluate my strengths and weaknesses and how I had done in reaching my goals. I turned it in to my boss three weeks before our meeting. When I showed up, it became clear that he had not looked at my report and had filled in his form in a hurry. All the ratings were average, and when I asked him how I could bring them up, he said he would have to think about it. Twenty minutes later he said he had another meeting. I had waited all year to get feedback from my boss, and when it finally came, it was almost meaningless. I have never felt so insignificant.

—Nursing supervisor, hospital

"What If I Don't Know How?"

Many managers are uncomfortable giving feedback (positive or negative) because they don't know how to do it simply and effectively. Many have never had a good role model. Giving feedback so that it doesn't put employees on the defensive is key. How do you measure up? Take the quiz in table 20.1 to see if you are feedback-savvy.

Table 20.1. Feedback quiz

MY FEEDBACK . . .		
is private.	____ True	____ False
receives the time it deserves.	____ True	____ False
is frequent.	____ True	____ False
focuses more on the future than the past.	____ True	____ False
is specific, with clear examples.	____ True	____ False
gives information that helps the person to make decisions.	____ True	____ False
gives suggestions for growth and improvement.	____ True	____ False
allows for discussion.	____ True	____ False
creates next steps.	____ True	____ False
preserves dignity.	____ True	____ False

How did you do? If most of these statements are true for you, fantastic! Now go ask your employees if they agree. Ask them to tell you the truth.

Good leaders respect diversity, which means considering various communication styles and points of view. Remember to take cultural as well as individual differences into account as you plan to give usable, valued feedback. And remember to *ask* people how they prefer to receive input from you.

T

In China we often go through a third party when giving feedback.
That's so the recipient can save face. It's hard to have a plain hon-
est conversation, given the power differential between boss and
employee. 坦诚相待

—Consultant in Singapore

Confidentially Speaking

Another popular approach is 360-degree feedback: employees receive
feedback from you, their peers, mentors, customers, and direct reports.
The feedback also includes a self-assessment that lets people compare
their own perceptions with the views of others. The 360-degree feedback highlights both strengths and opportunities to improve, and
its purpose is developmental. Because it is usually anonymous, raters
tend to be honest. It is valuable for all of us to get input from someone
other than the boss; this process is just one way of doing that.

Note: Be sure to follow up with coaching and support for people
who get critical feedback about behaviors they need to change. Getting the feedback is usually just the first step; most people will need
help creating and implementing a development plan.

Tell Them the Truth about the Organization

Research overwhelmingly supports the notion that engaged employees are "in the know." They want to be trusted with the truth about the
business, including its challenges and downturns.

We know, however, that there may be times when you are simply
not at liberty to tell the whole truth. A pending merger, reorganiza-
tion, or change at the top of the organization could be off-limits for
discussion with your team. Managers sometimes hold information
back in the belief that it makes them more powerful or that it is better
for their employees not to know. When you have bad news, give it face-
to-face and as soon as possible. If you make a mistake, confess, tell
people the truth, and accept responsibility. Your personal stock will go
up, and so will the trust level on your team.

Ask Them for the Truth (Even about You)

We would rather be ruined by praise then saved by criticism.

—Norman Vincent Peale

Many managers (especially at high levels) have had no formal performance reviews or feedback sessions for years. By the time they rise to the top, they might be getting almost no balanced, accurate input about how they get their work done. Often, leaders are rewarded as long as they hit their bottom-line targets.

Who, then, tells senior leaders about their warts? Probably no one. This is especially true in some cultures. Absence of truthful, balanced feedback creates leaders who have missed the opportunity to grow, to be even more effective in their jobs, and to keep their talented people.

In a weekly staff meeting, I told my employees I wanted feedback about my skills as a manager. I told them I'd had input that I could be better at delegation and employee development. I asked them to rate me on a 1–10 scale on each of those skills and then to tell me what I would need to do differently to be scored a 10. One person told me I was already a 10—that got a laugh from the group. We agreed they would type their responses and give them to my assistant. She delivered the anonymous responses to me, and I shared them with my group at the next staff meeting. They know what I'm working on and are willing to give me more feedback as I try to improve.

—Sales vice president, global biotech company

In almost every setting outside the modern organization, experts and masters continue to ask for the truth about their performance, and they strive for improvement. Athletes, musicians, and martial arts masters are examples of people who use honest feedback to refine their skills even more. Imagine what you, as a leader, could learn if your employees felt comfortable speaking up or pushing back. Imagine what that learning could do for you, your team, and your organization.

You can establish an environment where truth is welcome. And you can serve as a model for your employees as they watch how you seek and receive feedback. View the truth as a gift.

If You Manage Managers

On your organization's most recent satisfaction survey, employees asked (again) for more feedback about their performance, their strengths, and their weaknesses. How do we know that? Because it happens almost every time, in every industry and every country. For many reasons, the managers you manage may not be giving their talented people feedback honestly or often enough. Remind them, model it for them, and hold them accountable for ongoing, supportive, effective truth telling.

BOTTOM LINE

Talented people want to hear the truth about themselves and the organization. They need to feel free to tell you the truth as well. Honest feedback is a gift you can both give and receive. Truth telling can help keep your talented people engaged and growing. Tell—and hear—the truth.

CHAPTER TWENTY-ONE

Understand

LISTEN DEEPER

Ponder this: When you tune out, how do you miss out?

Why is there no end to the training courses on the subject of listening? Why do feedback surveys repeatedly tell managers that they are poor listeners? Why don't we get it? We might believe that listening is a critical skill and that we're already good at it. We don't need lessons or reminders. Or do we?

> *Ivan understands me. He listens to me—and I feel understood.*
> *The more he listens, the stronger our relationship becomes.*
> *We have developed a huge amount of trust. With other bosses,*
> *I used to edit. I tell Ivan everything. As a result, he is never sur-*
> *prised. He has a better handle on things. Because of our bond,*
> *we are more creative, take bigger risks, push the boundaries, and*
> *accomplish amazing things. I have never had a better boss, and*
> *I have never been so productive. Right now, nothing could entice*
> *me away from this job.*
>
> —Vice president, global engineering organization

Effective love 'em managers are all great listeners. Think back to your favorite bosses. Didn't they have this quality in common? They were genuinely *curious* about you. They listened to understand. They listened carefully to what you said—and even to what you didn't say. They wondered what you might want and need, and they helped you get that.

Listen aggressively. Listen attentively. Listen to the silence. Listen with your eyes. Listen!
—Bob Tiede, author of *Now That's a Great Question*

How are you doing in the listening department?

Write down three or four things you learned from your employees this week. It could be process improvement ideas they have, a customer (or family) challenge they face, or a team issue they struggle with. If you can't list three or four things you learned, you probably have not been listening carefully enough to your employees.

Communication is critical to keeping your talent. If people feel heard, understood, and valued by you, they will work harder and produce more. They will want to stay and work for you. And if they don't feel heard, they will disengage or depart.

Pay Attention, Please

You don't have to be interesting. You have to be interested.
—Dr. John Gottman, author and therapist

The manager's head moves up and down. She says, "Uh-huh," 16 times in a row. Is she listening? Maybe so, maybe not. What gets in the way of listening deeper? What are you thinking about while your employee talks?

Which of these do you sometimes think while your employees talk to you? Be honest.

★ I already know the punch line. I'm five steps ahead.

★ I'm too busy for this. I have a stack of work on my desk.

★ He's getting emotional. I'm checking out.

★ Now what should my response be? How can I defend my position?

★ She's so boring. I'm going to check my email while she talks.

★ That's not relevant.

★ You're so off target.

★ There's nothing new here.

★ We solved that a long time ago.

How did you do? You might believe that it is great time management (multitasking) to have your mind busy while another person talks or to be planning your response so that you are ready the minute the employee stops speaking. You might be impatient. Or you may have just forgotten how to really focus on a person and listen deeply. Regardless of your reason, the result is the same. *When you tune out, you miss out.* You miss out on information. More important, you miss out on having a respectful relationship.

> *Learn to listen. You don't learn anything from hearing yourself talk.*
>
> —Leo Buscaglia

The Blinking Word

Many managers are becoming better listeners by learning a simple technique called the *blinking word*. Here is how it works:

Scenario: Your employee, Shelby, asks to talk to you, so you schedule a meeting in your office. You welcome Shelby in and ask what you can do for her. She says, "I'm having **trouble** with one of my employees. He seems to **lack motivation** for the job."

1. Identify the words that blink (stand out). *"I'm having **trouble** with one of my employees. He seems to lack **motivation** for the job."*

2. Ask about one of the blinking words. *"What kind of trouble?"* or *"How does he seem to lack motivation?"*

3. Listen for Shelby's answer. *"He's not as **productive** as he used to be."*

4. Notice the blinking word in her answer and question it. *"How has his productivity dropped?"*

5. Listen for Shelby's answer. *"He gets less work done in a week, and the **quality has slipped** too."*

6. Notice the blinking words in her answer and question them. *"Why do you think he is getting less work done?"* or *"Tell me about the slip in quality."*

7. Keep going, watch for the blinking words, and ask about them.

U

Use open questions as you follow the blinking words. Open questions begin with words like *how, why, where, when,* and *tell me about.* They are designed to avoid yes or no responses, which often lead to a dead end. As you follow the blinking word, you go deeper into Shelby's problem.

Meanwhile, Shelby feels listened to. She believes that you care about her dilemma and are there to help her solve it. The blinking word technique will help you listen with *empathy.* When you do that, you identify with the feelings, thoughts, or attitudes of your employees. That takes you beyond listening and into understanding. And did you know that listening with empathy is the one thing robots can't yet do?

One manager asked, "What if I follow the wrong blinking word?" There's no such thing. Your employee will quickly correct course, redirect the conversation, and get you back on track.

You will not be able to tune in and out and still follow the blinking word. *Do* try this at home. Your spouse, kids, and friends will be pleasantly surprised at what a good listener you have become.

ALAS

I watched him read his email while his employees talked to him. I was on the receiving end of that behavior a few times myself. He probably thought we didn't notice or that we respected his ability to multitask. He was wrong. We felt unimportant and unheard most of the time.

—Frontline employee

Listening Is a Choice

You might already have great listening skills and habits, but you may be selective about when you use them. Be conscious about how you are listening to your employees. Listen with a wide-angle lens—more expansively than before. Narrow the focus sometimes and listen deeper. Take your curiosity to the conversation. Ask, "What do you think?"

The greatest compliment that was ever paid me was when one
asked me what I thought and attended to my answer.
—Henry David Thoreau

Sometimes you've got to see the reason for better listening. One executive said that when he worked in Japan, he found a reason and he learned to really listen. The reason was comprehension. He was listening so intently and striving to truly understand what people were trying to convey. He was not listening so that he could critique or object or convince.

Listening to understand helps you get information you need to be effective as a manager. It's a form of field research and gives you crucial signals from your ecosystem. In the process, you're showing respect to the people doing the talking.

Listen Up

Experts have been writing about the importance of listening in the world of work forever. Still, leaders who don't listen remain one of the biggest complaints on the part of employees everywhere. Kenny Moore, in *The CEO and the Monk*, suggests that listening has become a lost art in business.

Become a better communicator by keeping your mouth shut. . . .
We risk creating a culture where the ones that speak the most
and the loudest win out. My instincts tell me that that's not going
to satisfy our customers, whether external or internal. There is
something to be said for maintaining a quiet demeanor. Silence
on our part invites the thoughts and opinions of others, a true
recipe for sustained growth and competitive advantage."[1]

WAIT!

Why

Am

I

Talking?

—Al-Anon.org

U

If you notice you're talking more than you're listening, try doing the opposite. It will take practice and patience (and feedback from those around you) to make the change, but you'll find it worth the effort.

Diversity, Inclusion, and Listening Effectively

What does listening effectively have to do with diversity and inclusion? Without effective communication, verbal and nonverbal, it's difficult, if not impossible, to be an inclusive leader.

How do you listen to those who are different in the following areas?

★ **Style.** Your talented people could include those who are succinct versus rambling, outgoing versus shy, soft talkers versus loud talkers. They have something to say to you, even though they'll say it differently.

★ **Accents.** Consider the differences as you listen to employees from Ireland or Iran, Brazil or Belarus, Texas or Tacoma. It sometimes takes practice to effectively hear what they tell you.

★ **Generation.** The language you speak (and write) can vary between people from different generations. For example, your grandfather's English can be somewhat different from your own.

Boomer or Gen Z: Which group said #1 below? Which said #2? (Ask your grandma and your grandson for help.)

1. *I'm woke . . . can't believe what's happening to them at this time. By the way, you are slaying it with that haircut. Look at him in his new car . . . just flexing . . . could be lit.*

2. *Don't sweat it if you can't hang loose with us. Not everyone is hot to trot on such a tough challenge. But if you know how to get your groove on, we'll wager you can get it done.*

Notice your biases and preferences as you learn to listen deeply. Put judgment aside; listen, ask for clarification, and listen again. Try to find the meaning behind someone's words. It could even be fun to learn a *new* language.

Listening can fuel a company culture of respect. That culture becomes a talented-people magnet. People will want to work for you and your organization, and they'll recruit their friends.

Listening Liabilities

You want to be a better listener; we all do. Which of the behaviors in table 21.1 might prevent you from really *hearing* what your employees have to say?

Table 21.1. Listening liabilities

MY LISTENING LIABILITIES	YES	NO	MAYBE
Interrupting			
Defending my point of view			
Transmitting (talking) more than listening			
Drifting (mind wandering while they talk)			
Derailing (steering conversations to what interests me more)			
Rambling versus being succinct			
Opinion-giving (especially when not solicited)			
Multitasking			
Biased listening (based on age, culture, title, gender, personality, etc.)			

How'd you do? Awareness of your listening liabilities is the first step toward correcting them. Pick one or two to work on. Get feedback about your progress. Be patient; some of these behaviors are habitual for you, and it will take some time to replace them with more effective listening behaviors.

Beware of the Put-Down

If you haven't said these things, you've no doubt heard them:

★ That's not relevant.

★ You've got to be kidding.

★ This is all you have?

★ That makes no sense.

U

★ You're off target.

★ There's nothing new here.

★ We solved that a long time ago.

★ I can't believe you didn't know that.

How does it feel when you're on the receiving end of these put-downs? Demoralizing? Disrespectful? Notice if—or when—you accidentally deploy one of these weapons. Catch yourself and correct course.

Listen Deeper

Every person I work with knows something better than I—
my job is to listen long enough to find it and use it.
                          —Jack Nicklaus, champion golfer

Some managers wonder, "What should I be listening for?" We believe it is important to listen for the following:

★ *Input.* Talented people want you to have an ear for their great ideas and solutions. They want to be heard and recognized.

★ *Motivations.* What do they want from this job and from you? What gets them up in the morning and looking forward to their work?

★ *Challenges.* You need to know about your employees' obstacles.

Some of our readers have said they are uncomfortable listening deeply, especially about employees' lives outside work. They fear heartfelt conversations may take them to a personal level or an empathetic state that leaves them vulnerable.

Some managers don't want their people to discuss their personal lives at all. I say, bring it on. If people can get something off their chest for an hour, I've got them for the next 20 (or more).
                          —Team leader, small manufacturing plant

*I hire knowledge workers. I need their brainpower. If they are
unhappy with me, the organization, or their personal lives, they
show up at work with half a brain. I can't afford that. I listen to
their problems, help them brainstorm solutions, and refer them
to helpful resources. I work very hard to keep them happy.*
                                    —Executive, German high-tech company

You don't have to play counselor, and you don't have to have answers to employees' personal problems. Just listen.

If You Manage Managers

Engage the managers you manage in a listening challenge for a month.
Find out which listening tips and tricks work best for you and for
them. Have managers make their own specific commitments. After
a month, ask them to get feedback from employees. Has anything
shifted? What if everyone who works to improve this skill sees results?

BOTTOM LINE

Get to know your people. Make time to understand them by really listening to them. Notice your own listening style and improve it (there's
always room). Your efforts will pay off. Employees who feel heard and
understood will stay engaged and on your team. Those who don't will
find another place to work with a boss who will listen.

U

CHAPTER TWENTY-TWO

Values

DEFINE AND MINE

Ponder this: What do they really value most?

Values define what we consider to be important. They are the standards for measuring our bottom-line needs. And more than anything, they are the engine for our actions. They help us decide how much of ourselves we bring to our work and whether we should stay—or leave for a job that delivers on what matters most.

Values are unique to you, and they are unique to every one of your talented people. How will you know if those on your team are getting what they value most? And what might you do with the information you receive?

You can help your talented people clearly *define* their values and then *mine* (search for) ways their work can deliver on those values. If you do that, you'll increase the odds that your people will stay engaged and on your team—for a little while longer.

> *Values are the emotional salary of work, and some folks are drawing no wages at all.*
> —Howard Figler, author of *The Complete Job Search Handbook*

Leadership expert and author Jim Kouzes says that values influence every aspect of our lives, including moral judgments, commitments to personal and organizational goals, and even the way we respond to others. They inform priority-setting and decision-making. And they help explain choices we make. We seldom act on options that conflict with our value system. If we do, it's with a sense of compliance rather than commitment.[1]

Values Go to Work

Whether you're 26 or 66, male or female, light skinned or dark, and whether you work in Detroit, Dublin, or Dubai, you take your values with you every day. They help you perform and excel. And it's best when they match up with the work you've agreed to do.

Conflicts over values increase the risk of losing employees far more than conflicts over pay. People want to spend time doing something they truly value. So how will you learn about what they value most? Ask.

Try some of these questions:

★ Which parts of your job give you the greatest satisfaction?

★ What do you need most from your work? Does the job deliver?

★ What makes for a really good day?

★ What would you miss if you left this job?

★ What did you like best about other jobs you've had?

★ What small steps can we take to increase the value proposition for you in this job?

★ Can you tell me about a time when you really felt energized at work?

★ How do your values match to mine or the team's or the organization's values?

★ What might we do to better align those values?

As people answer, probe for specifics. Does "a good day" mean having more customer contact, giving a speech, leading a task force, or helping a new employee get settled on the team?

My work is often physically difficult. I leave work exhausted but with a smile on my face. You see, I get to help over a dozen elderly patients every single day. I help them with the activities of daily living—but I also help them find joy in their day. I make a point to visit, to ask about their families, to read cards and letters they've received. I could make more money and do less strenuous work in another career. But I love helping people. This job is all about helping.

—Nurse aide in the Philippines

→ **TRY THIS**

At your next one-on-ones, show your employees the following list of value choices. Ask which five matter most. Are they getting those in their work? Listen to their responses and ask another question. If they're not getting what they value, ask how you might help them get more of that. Remember to follow the blinking word (see Understand). Suggest they add to the list.

1. Holding a position of formal authority
2. Pursuing an interest outside of work
3. Working in a supportive and harmonious setting
4. Doing challenging work
5. Being well-liked
6. Having autonomy and independence
7. Doing meaningful work
8. Working on a variety of tasks
9. Having high earnings potential
10. Working in a specific geographical location
11. Focusing on personal growth
12. Taking risks
13. Having control over my time and schedule
14. Being creative or innovative
15. Competing
16. Having fun at work
17. Having stability
18. Dedicating time to serving my community
19. Learning continuously
20. Having prestige and status
21. Pursuing spiritual development
22. Solving complex problems
23. Being recognized
24. Being responsible for important projects
25. Spending time with family and/or friends
26. Working with people who are different from me

V

Values and Diversity

There are at least two connections we can make between the words *values* and *diversity*.

First, *diversity of values* will build strength on your team. How?

★ Those who value creativity can be your innovators.

★ Those who value independence might work productively for long stretches without prodding from you.

★ Those who value order and routine could be your dependable, solid citizens.

★ Those who value respect for others might help you build a more respectful team.

★ Those who value life outside of work might teach others about work-life balance.

★ Those who use silence effectively could coach those who value speaking up—and vice-versa.

★ Those who value different views can support those who are often cut off when they offer fresh ideas.

(Those who value perfection can be our copy editors.)
Second, *valuing diversity* will build strength on your team.

→ TRY THIS:

★ Check your own list of values. Is "working with people who are different from you" on that list? You might say yes, but realize you could do more.

★ Take a good look at your team and ask yourself (and them), "How diverse and inclusive are we now? How might we recruit and include more people who think, look, and speak differently from us? And why would we do that?"

When you really value something, you want more of that—for yourself, your employees, your family, your world. Valuing and leveraging differences could make your team the best it's ever been.

Values Gaps

Where is the connection (or disconnect) between your employees' values and their work or workplace? Why should it matter? A global study found the top three employee satisfaction predictors to be as follows:[2]

1. Alignment with the culture and *values* of the organization

2. The quality of senior leadership

3. Access to career opportunities within the organization

Values connections at every level lead to employee satisfaction, which leads to engagement and retention. Sadly, management sometimes appears to expect employees to ignore their personal values in favor of the ones posted on the wall. When employee values clash with the organization's, the outcome is often disengagement and, ultimately, departure of talent.

Speaking of the values posted on the wall: have you noticed there is sometimes a difference between espoused values and practiced values?

ALAS

The company values list hangs in the boardroom, the conference room, and the lunchroom. It's a great list, but I began to distrust it. The first sentence said, "We value employees more than anything else." I loved reading that when I first joined the company. I loved finding a company where loyalty and commitment were a two-way street and highly valued. Now I don't believe in the list on the wall. We have regular layoffs, mostly to deliver to shareholders. The list should read, "We value shareholders more than anything else."

—Disenchanted (disengaged) employee

Your employees don't look to marketing brochures or wall posters to determine company values. They watch leadership behavior. Who and what do you reward? Punish? Where is money invested? They look to the culture you and other leaders create and support to assess what is truly valued and what is not.

Talk with them about any values gaps they feel exist and truly *mine* for solutions. For example, corporate philanthropy or social responsibility programs matter greatly to some. When you learn that's the case, link people to existing company projects, or support their finding or starting one themselves. If these talented employees are proud of what their organization does in the community, their engagement levels can soar.

What Have *You* Got to Do with It?

We have looked at hundreds of transcripts from exit interviews. We were amazed at how many talented employees left because their values conflicted with those of their immediate supervisor or manager.

Tom's top value was clear to everyone—to his boss, his peers, and his team. He valued bottom-line results and delivering on promises—at any cost, including frequent sacrifices in his personal life. He managed a group of millennials who expected both a great job and a great life. After discussing the values gap in a staff meeting, Tom and his team realized they needed to get creative and to somehow reconcile that gap. Here are the steps Tom took:

1. *Met with every team member to get clear about what mattered most to each one*

2. *Asked each of them to bring suggestions for closing the values gap to the next meeting*

3. *Crafted tangible work agreements with each team member*

4. *Agreed to discuss progress and revise agreements over the coming weeks and months*

5. *Committed to keep working until the values gap was closed*

One agreement entailed flexing the work schedule so an employee could attend his son's rugby matches. In another case, Tom clarified the performance objectives, gained agreement with the employee—then let go, allowing her to manage her own workload in her own way. One by one, Tom and his talented employees tested the new agreements, modified them where necessary, and, in time, closed the values gaps. It wasn't as difficult as Tom thought it would be—and it was worth the effort. His team is happier and more productive than ever before.

Are you aware of the values gaps you may have with those on your team?

Values on Display

How do your talented people really know what you value? They watch, they listen, and they see how you show up and how you act, especially in tough times.

One of my terrific employees, Mo, was due home from a month-long visit to his home country in Africa. Now he is stuck there, unable to return because of the coronavirus. I told him it was too risky to fly to New York City and that he should stay in Africa for a month or two, however long it takes for this virus threat to diminish. I offered to take care of all his expenses, like rent, flights home, child support, truck payment, whatever he needs. He said, "Thank you. I love you." I said, "I love you too, man; anything you need, we're here for you."

I really try to communicate well with my employees and my customers. I set up a process we call a group hug. *It means let's make a plan, or let's talk about what's going on and how we can help each other. I learned to appreciate my employees' differences and to value and use the gift each brings to my team. I try to train them well and then let go and let them work more independently. I'm here for them in good and bad times. So this turned out to be a very challenging time for Mo, and I was here for him—and he knew that.*

—Justin Smith, owner/operator of
Potter Plumbing Inc., California

Justin's employees know what he values. Why? Because he lives them.

V

→ TRY THIS

Talk about values (again) with your team. Here are some questions that might get the conversation rolling and spark a meaningful conversation about diversity and inclusion:

★ What are the values we have individually? How are we similar? How are we different?

★ How might our differences get in the way? Or help pave the way?

★ Under what circumstances or pressures do we find our values colliding? Complementing?

★ What can we learn from someone whose values are different from our own?

★ Do we have espoused or practiced team values? How do they show up? Help us? Hinder us?

★ Should we spend a little time in every meeting talking about where we're "on" or "off" our values? If not, why not?

★ How might we close the values gaps we discover?

If You Manage Managers

Does your organization have a published set of values hanging on a wall somewhere? In your annual report? On your website? Ask your managers if they feel these are the values your organization espouses or actually practices. Discuss the values they believe are alive and well in your own department. And ask what you can do, in concert with them, to reconcile any values gaps. Hold them accountable for delivering on and modeling agreed-upon values, and ask them to do the same with their talented people.

BOTTOM LINE

Finding creative ways to deliver on values is a powerful factor in keeping good people. How satisfied are they with their everyday tasks? What do they love about working in your organization? What do they wish would change? Do you know enough about your employees' values to answer these questions? Values may be difficult to uncover, but they are worth the effort. They are powerful forces in an employee's decision to stay or leave. Imagine your employees as your customers. What do they value most? How can you help them attain it?

CHAPTER TWENTY-THREE

Wellness

SUSTAIN IT

Ponder this: Are they sick or tired?

Companies that take wellness seriously find that the payoff is great, not only in retention, but also in energy for the job and in productivity. But this chapter is not about what the corporation can do. We are interested in how you, the manager, can enhance your team's wellness.

What are *you* doing to encourage the wellness of your talented people?

Wellness and Survival of the Fit

Today's workplace is typically high-energy and highly productive. To play successfully within it, you and your employees must be *well and fit*—mentally, emotionally, and physically. In this competitive environment, wellness is a "must have" rather than a "nice to have." Without it, you simply will not win. By focusing on your employees' wellness, you can increase the odds that they will stay and play effectively on your team.

"I don't have a wellness budget." That's what we hear from managers who want healthy employees but assume that costs a lot (think gymnasiums, volleyball courts, stress management classes). It doesn't have to. Here are some low-cost solutions we've heard of:

★ Healthy snacks

★ Walking meetings

★ Water cooler on your floor

★ Treadmill in the conference room

★ Standing/walking desks

★ Plants in the office

★ Health library: books and articles

★ Stair-climbing challenges (ring a bell at the top)

★ Group outings to take a break

★ Laugh breaks—bring a joke to work

★ Fitness challenges: partnering or teaming

★ Siesta closets—for that power nap

What Is Wellness?

To one person, *wellness* means being able to enter the Dead Sea Marathon and finish in four hours. To another, it may mean finally being free of migraine headaches. To another, it may mean slimming down or reducing stress and high blood pressure before the next physical exam.

We define *wellness* as a "state of physical, mental, and emotional fitness." Some might call it *well-being*. To capture a clear picture of it, you might need to think back to a recent vacation when you felt incredibly relaxed, physically healthy and energetic, mentally sharp (maybe even creative), and emotionally satisfied. It may seem unreasonable to expect that you or your employees will feel at work like you feel on vacation, but it is useful to have the "perfect world" scenario in mind as you strive to increase your employees' fitness and wellness levels.

Notice if something is wrong or if your employees' work habits change dramatically. Do not wait. Ask how you might help and then collaborate on a plan. Take individual differences into account; wellness strategies for one person will not necessarily work for another.

→ TRY THIS

★ Notice your employees. Listen to them: pay attention to what they say—or don't say.

★ Be aware of the signals you send through your tone of voice, attitude, word selection, body language, and even timing of the conversation. These signals say more than words alone can say.

★ Have an open-door policy. Encourage employees to stop by to vent, share ideas, and more.

★ Empathize. Let them know you hear them, care about them, and have their backs.

The "B" Word (Balance)

Most of us need a job, and all of us want a life. We should be able to have both.

A senior executive lamented, "I haven't called my mother in a month, and I'm six months overdue for a mammogram. Both issues weigh on my mind and increase my stress." Workers want a break, and they want a life outside work. They want time to call Mom and get a checkup.

Balance between one's work and personal life contributes to wellness and constantly challenges the wellness-minded manager. One team we know has spent so much time in recent years dealing with the issue of balance that they now call it the "B" word. It is almost off-limits as a discussion topic because it seems there are few solutions, and they have become "sick of talking about it."

We believe, though, that you *need to talk about it*—and think about it—and even do something about it!

Defining Work-Life Balance

What does balance mean to you and to your employees? It is different for everyone. Why? Because balance needs or preferences are influenced by dozens of variables, such as culture, upbringing, responsibilities outside of work, health, energy, personality, emotion, family position or structure, geography, habitat, climate, age, gender, ethnicity, hobbies, sports, and occupation.

How will you ever guess which of these influencers are true for any of your talented people? You won't. You'll ask. You'll ask what balance means to them and how you might partner with them to get more of it, right where they are.

We are not suggesting that your employees' balance issues are your concern alone or that you must provide the answers. We are

W

suggesting, however, that you can take actions to encourage balance and thus wellness.

> *Imagine life as a game in which you are juggling some five balls in the air. You name them—work, family, health, friends, and spirit—and you're keeping all of these in the air. You will soon understand that work is a rubber ball. If you drop it, it will bounce back. But the other four balls—family, health, friends, and spirit— are made of glass. If you drop one of these, it will be irrevocably scuffed, marked, nicked, damaged, or even shattered. They will never be the same. You must understand that.*
>
> —Brian Dyson, former CEO, Coca-Cola

Overwhelm Is an Understatement

Do more with less. Move faster than the competition. Be more creative, more innovative, more distinct. Do it with fewer dollars. Be available at all times. These pressures push many to say that work just asks too much.

In the United States and many other parts of the world, the workweek keeps getting longer in the hopes of creating a competitive advantage. That's in spite of decades of research that confirms that "the 'sweet spot' is 40 hours a week—and that while adding another 20 hours provides a minor increase in productivity, that increase only lasts for three to four weeks, *and then turns negative.*" The good news is that in 6 of the top 10 most competitive countries in the world (Sweden, Finland, Germany, the Netherlands, Denmark, and the UK), it's *illegal* to demand more than a 48-hour workweek.[1]

ALAS

Kumar noticed he was snapping at his employees, having trouble sleeping, and feeling generally sluggish. When a friend asked him how he was spending his time away from work, he answered, "What time away from work?" He used to work out regularly and enjoyed movies, friends, books, and music. All of that seemed a distant memory. His new boss set the tone: those who are even remotely ambitious or committed to the organization work late every night. Kumar finally began to check out internet job postings, thinking there must be a saner place to work! He found that place, where balance is at least a topic of discussion and his new boss expects that people have a life outside work.

What about you? What example do you set as a manager, and what do you expect from your people? Ask yourself these questions:

★ Do I promote workaholism? Am I a workaholic?

★ Do I expect my employees to travel or work on weekends? How often?

★ Do I hold numerous early morning or evening meetings?

★ Do I compliment employees for their long hours or, instead, for the quality work they complete?

How did you do? Often managers discourage balance by the examples they set or by what they expect and reward.

→ TRY THIS

★ Set the example you want others to follow. If you want them to have more balance in their lives, model it. Share what you do to achieve balance in your life, or your employees may think that you have none. (We hope they're wrong.)

★ Hold a balance discussion at your next staff meeting (or in one-on-one meetings). Dedicate the whole meeting to the topic.

★ Ask people what they juggle in their lives and what matters most to them. Listen to the diversity of answers, and be ready to hear that work is *not the number-one priority* for some.

★ Support your employees in achieving balance. Encourage the activities that they love; ask about their golf lessons or their children's school plays.

W

Stretched and Stressed

I used up all my sick days so I called in dead.

—Anonymous

Hans Selye, the founder of the field of stress management, said, "Complete freedom from stress is death."[2] We agree that just *living* is often stressful. But Selye and others have found that although optimum levels of stress produce peak performance, overdoses can definitely lead to poor performance and even to illness.

In organizations, we seldom see too little stress. We sometimes see the optimum stress level, resulting in high performance. Most often, however, we see stress overload and negative results on health and productivity. There seems to be a high correlation between lack of balance and stress. Where balance is missing, the workload typically appears to be very high and stressful. When people have balanced lives, they seem to have less work stress, or they just manage it better.

> *For 40 years, we focused, as a medical profession, on the deleterious effects of stress. We now know that with people who are stressed, there is a direct correlation with addictive behavior, cardiovascular disease, infections and some types of cancer. But we hadn't looked at the opposite. If stress could make you sick, could happiness make you better? And the evidence shows it can.*
>
> —Deepak Chopra

Both Switzerland and France have labor laws that protect employees' health and wellness. Swiss law prescribes the "duty of care," where companies are not allowed to accept or create a work environment that is hostile to employees' health. Meanwhile, French employers must ensure the physical and mental health of employees. This includes taking measures against any psychological suffering and stress. Employers must therefore remove unrealistic deadlines and heavy workloads. In turn, they must ensure that employees have control over their own workloads and schedules.

Perhaps you manage in a country that has no such laws. There are still many ways that you, as an individual manager, can promote a healthy work environment.

→ **TRY THIS**

★ Watch for signs of excess stress. When you think you see it in your employees, ask them how they are doing (or feeling). They will appreciate your asking and may confide in you.

★ Once you know what's going on, brainstorm possible solutions with your employees. Be open and willing to think creatively as you search for ways to relieve stress and increase well-being.

★ Support your employees as they practice stress management. For example, if Phil decides he needs to take two 15-minute brisk walks during the day to relieve stress, be sure that you reward his actually doing it. Your support will pay off.

★ Take a good look at the role you play. Stop calling your employees in the evening—give them a break.

When we create a desirable workplace and find good ways to have work-life balance, we'll attract and we'll retain the best people—and that's our competitive advantage.
                    —Lewis Platt, former CEO, Hewlett-Packard

Small Steps to Big Change

Which of the following actions are you taking to reduce stress? Which might you try? You go first—then pass on the ideas to your talented people (and your boss).

★ Shift some of the work to others if possible. Think about who could help and how to ask for the help.

★ Take more breaks. Get up; move around; go for a quick walk.

★ Take a break from "electronic leashes"—declare a smart-phone-free Wednesday morning (unless that increases others' stress!).

★ Learn relaxation, visualization, or breathing techniques. Take a stress management or mindfulness class.

★ Exercise as a way to relieve stress. Join a gym or take up power walking, yoga, or jogging.

★ Implement "no meetings on Fridays." Think of the work you could get done!

W

★ Seek professional help or counseling.

★ Sleep and eat. How long has it been since you took a lunch break—away from your desk?

★ Take a vacation—a real one.

★ Practice gratitude. Every day, picture and list the things you are grateful for. Your family, friends, colleagues, work, home, dog? You can't help but smile.

What about Burnout?

Burnout is stress that is specific to one's work versus other life stressors. The term *burnout* originated in the 1970s, and the phenomenon is now considered by many as a global workplace epidemic.

Author and workplace consultant Jennifer Moss explains the phenomenon:

> *In 2019 the World Health Organization (WHO) included burnout in its International Classification of Diseases, conveying to the world that burnout would be recognized explicitly as a workplace phenomenon.[3] It may not seem significant to some, but this designation has the potential to dramatically impact organizations globally. Why? Because it finally acknowledges that burnout is a workplace problem, not an employee problem.*

Burnout is a syndrome conceptualized as resulting from chronic workplace stress that has not been successfully managed. Burnout has three dimensions:

★ Feelings of energy depletion or exhaustion

★ Increased mental distance from one's job, or feelings of negativism or cynicism related to one's job

★ Reduced professional efficacy[4]

And burnout is expensive! Stanford University professor Jeffrey Pfeffer, author of *Dying for a Paycheck*, says "there are 120,000 excess deaths per year attributed to . . . workplace conditions and they cause approximately $190 billion in incremental healthcare costs. That would make the workplace the fifth leading cause of death in the U.S. higher than Alzheimer's, higher than kidney disease."[5]

So why might your employee have burnout? A Gallup study determined the top five reasons for burnout to be the following:[6]

1. Unfair treatment at work

2. Unmanageable workload

3. Lack of role clarity

4. Lack of communication and support from the manager

5. Unreasonable time pressure

Given the causes outlined here, the solutions would seem evident. And many of them are in your hands. Treat people fairly, don't overload them, be clear about their roles, communicate and support them, and stop the unreasonable pressure.

If you suspect burnout, ask your employees how they feel and what they need. Then take action on their behalf.

If You Manage Managers

Take a stand to increase wellness on your team. Coach the managers who report to you. Reward and hold them accountable for reducing, not increasing, the stress of their workers. Caring about employees' well-being should not be an afterthought. It is central to the role of a manager and belongs in the top line of the position description.

BOTTOM LINE

Savvy managers view work-life balance and stress reduction initiatives as strategic business tools, not employee perks. If your employees are well and feel a balance between work and life outside work, you are far more likely to have a well-functioning organization. Your best employees will work hard, produce for you, *and stick around* in an environment that promotes their emotional, mental, and physical health and fitness.

W

CHAPTER TWENTY-FOUR

X-plore Generations

BEWARE AND BE AWARE

Ponder this: How does understanding generations help you manage individuals?

Beware of stereotyping—but be aware of differences.

Imagine this dialogue between a manager (you) and the authors (us):

You: Why would you write a chapter that divides or labels people?

Us: Good question. The last thing we want to do is divide people. We do know that it is often helpful to understand differences to better serve or manage them.

You: Don't define me by my generation. I was born after 2000 and I have an extensive Elvis collection.

Us: We get it. We often want the same things because we're all human. Yet there are differences—cultural, generational, gender, and more. We suggest you embrace and value these differences and use them to better understand your talented people's motivations and goals.

The primary value of generational analysis is to make the actions of others a little more understandable. By understanding other generations' perspectives, we are better able to position our ideas and requests in ways that are likely to have positive results and avoid at least some of the frustrations of today's workplace.

. . . As you work with people from other generations and other backgrounds, think about their formative years for clues about why they may see things differently than you do.

—Tamara Erickson, generational expert and author

What's a Generation?

A *generation* is a group of people who share birth years and therefore life stages. Generations are defined by spikes and declines in birthrates. The people in those groups are influenced by the cultural events, changes, and challenges that they experience, especially during their formative years. As a result, they bring their own set of attitudes, perceptions, and values to the workplace.

To be part of a generation is much more than the simple matter of your birthday. It's to be a part of an era. It's to have fallen in love with a rock band and not a big band. Or to have played ball with an aluminum bat instead of a wooden one. It's to have done things as no other generation would.

—Unknown

Today's workplace contains five distinct generations, each bringing its own perspective and expectations. No wonder we have plenty of opportunities for generation gaps! The birth dates and population of each group vary slightly, depending on whose research you are using. We used Pew Research Center's definitions.[1] We suggest you worry less about the generational labels and dates and instead ask yourself, "How are the generations different—or similar? And how can that knowledge help me engage them and keep them in my organization?"

My grandmother collected paper bags—lots of them. She also "stole" sugar packets from every restaurant she went to. I was young and curious, so I asked her about her large supply of sacks and sugar. She explained that she grew up in the Great Depression and WWII. She said, "Everything was rationed and we all learned to stock up." I learned about her but also about her generation and what they lived through.

—Boomer

This chapter is based on US generational data. Readers in other countries might have different generational birth years and names from those you see here. What we all have in common, though, is generational differences in the workplace. As you read this chapter, think about how the characteristics of different age groups impact how work gets done in your organization.

Thanks to generational experts Devon Scheef and Diane Thielfoldt, from the Learning Café, for sharing your years of experience and research on this topic![2]

How Are We Similar? Count the Ways.

Many Millennials are lazy. Many others are not. Many others are sometimes lazy and sometimes not, and many others are lazy about certain things and not lazy about other things. The same can be said for any stereotype applied to any generation.
   —Jennifer J. Deal, author of *Retiring the Generation Gap*

We're not millennials, but Jennifer's quote fits for us too. Before we look at differences between generational groups, let's remember what we have in common. Most of us want respect, meaningful work, and recognition for work well done. We want credible, trustworthy leaders who know how to listen and who truly care about us. We want to be treated fairly and to have equal pay for equal work. We want to learn and grow. We want to have friends, colleagues, and family members to love. We want to have some fun at work—and in life.

Keep in mind that generations are a lens through which to understand societal change, rather than a label with which to oversimplify difference between groups.
   —Michael Dimock, president, Pew Research Center

After researching and partnering with the experts, here is what we've learned about the five generations in the workplace.

X

Generation Z (1997–2012)

Gen Z is the side hustle generation. The goal isn't necessarily to either own your own company or go work at one—the goal is to do both. Learning to program on the side is a perfect side hustle as Gen Z can do their full-time jobs with some programming on the side.

—Jonah Stillman, Gen Z guru

Slow to gather momentum around a name, Generation Z was initially referred to as the Next Gen, iGen, or postmillennnials. Gen Z has now taken hold, and with 72 million in this group, it will soon be the largest generation in the US workforce. It is also the most ethnically and racially diverse generation in the nation's history.

When the oldest Gen-Zers turned 10, the iPhone was introduced. The technology that previous generations remember as a big deal was just *how it is* for Gen Z—internet, computers, and (yawn) television. By the time they reached their teens, their primary means of connection were mobile devices, Wi-Fi, and high-bandwidth cellular. They consumed social media, constant connectivity, and on-demand entertainment. They grew up in an "always-on" environment.

Gen Z knows the power that ordinary people have to create instant community or effect change daily. Social technology is deeply embedded and has transformed how they interact, learn, and are entertained. The use of that technology makes Gen Z feel like anything is possible or attainable.

Gen-Zers bring a pragmatic view to work. Their youth was marked by post-9/11, the Great Recession, school shootings, climate-induced natural disasters, and the coronavirus pandemic. The ensuing chaos, volatility, and complexity require coping skills and resourcefulness.

They didn't experience the anything-is-possible-if-you-want-it parenting (like the millennials). They face an uncertain financial future, and their practical Gen X parents encourage them to be focused, prepared, and realistic. As they mature, they're expected to seek stability and security.

What They Bring and What They Want

Remember to ask each Gen-Zer what will keep him or her. Focus on individual preferences and then get curious about these generational observations. Which of the following ring true for your talented employees? Which ring true for you, even if you're in a different age group?

★ **Technology *and* human connection.** While a fan of collaboration tools, Gen-Zers want human connection too. Given that technology is in their DNA, we might imagine they always prefer virtual communication. To the contrary, many Gen-Zers say they prefer in-person communication. Few believe that technology enhances personal or professional relationships.

★ **Inclusion.** They are the most diverse generation in the United States, and they place great value on inclusion, for themselves and for others. In fact, that is just "how it's always been" for many if not most of them. Help them find people and groups that resonate with their personal values.

★ **Mentoring and learning.** Savvy Gen-Zers are entering the workplace with a realistic sensibility. Some bring experience gained through part-time jobs and internships. They look for work environments that foster mentoring, learning, and professional development. Realistic about how success is attained both personally and at work, they desire cred-building education and experience.

★ **Feedback—now!** They prioritize feedback—not only more frequent but also measurable. They are used to getting feedback from their video games and might expect their boss could do better in that department. Can they track progress on a scorecard? Do they impact an important company metric? Let them know, visually and often. *Often* means multiple times a week, not once a month or, heaven forbid, twice annually during the company performance review process.

★ **Brand clarity.** The "why" of work—meaning and purpose—really does matter to Gen Z. And those things are personal. Highly savvy about consumer brands, Gen-Zers understand that they,

X

too, are a brand at work. They know all about your organization's brand. To win their hearts, highlight authentic commitment to broader societal challenges—climate change, sustainability, social justice.

Millennials (1981–1996)

Every generation brings something new to the workplace, and millennials are no exception. As a group, they tend to be highly educated, love to learn, and grew up with the internet and digital tools in a way that can be highly useful when leveraged properly.
—Kathryn Minshew, cofounder and CEO,
The Muse

Millennials are also known as Gen Y or the echo boomers. With 71 million in this group, they are the largest generation in the US labor force. One-third of all workers are millennials.

They're the new MBAs, the new moms and dads, the new home-owners with a mortgage and college debt. They could be your assistant, coworker, or boss. While they have an undeserved generational reputation as job hoppers, they actually stay in roles for an average of three years and may take several roles within a single company.

They're ambitious, they know what they want, and they question everything, so if there isn't a good reason for that long commute or late night, don't expect them to do it. When it comes to loyalty, the companies they work for are last on their list—behind their families, their friends, their communities, their coworkers, and, of course, themselves.

And they might even want to bring their parents to work. Really? Yes. Some companies are even hosting *bring your parents to work days*.[3] But you don't need to wait for your company. You can provide an opportunity for parents to see firsthand what their kids do at work and to ask questions about everything from the 401(k) plan to stock purchasing options.

What They Bring and What They Want

Which of the following ring true for your talented millennials? Which ring true for you, even if you're in a different age group?

★ **Constant connection.** Millennials are digital natives, the first "always connected" generation. They've grown up with cell phones, laptops, broadband, and their own digital social networks. Not only do they have tricked-out laptops and digital devices; they might have a spare bedroom full of technology to power their second business as a solopreneur. They are great multitaskers. They're hard workers and used to meeting high expectations. They appreciate structure, process, and feedback.

★ **Work-life balance.** Simply waving money in the faces of millennials as a hiring tool is often a futile effort. They value experiences over stuff. They want the money but on their own terms: flexibility, good hours, a good work climate, and a job that offers opportunities to learn, grow, and have real responsibilities. Bottom line: they want *cool*, leading-edge careers that make a difference in the world.

★ **Team work and globalization.** Many prefer group activities to individual pursuits. They're great team players. They are tolerant of authority, welcome diversity, and are the best-educated generation in US history. This group is also the best prepared for globalization. They've always had access to world news (CNN was born about the same time they were), they've loved Pokémon cards along with kids from Japan, they've found a McDonald's restaurant in every country they've visited, and they have surely communicated with people from other countries on the net, one way or another.

★ **Feedback.** Give them regular, honest feedback. They grew up providing reviews (think Yelp and Amazon). The free flow of information makes sense to them. Their early years had schedules, tests, and constant input from tutors, teachers, parents, and coaches. They want feedback early, honestly, and often.

★ **Opportunities, clear goals, and kudos.** Help them create stretch goals, multiple career options, and a sense of belonging at work. Remind them of the many opportunities they have in your organization. And remember to recognize them when they achieve their goals—in ways that matter most to them (reward, comp time, bonus, visibility, learning).

X

Generation X (1965–1980)

Yo, Corporate America! I want a fat salary, a signing bonus, and a
cappuccino machine—oh, and I'm bringing my bird to work. I'm
the New Organization Man. You need me.

—1998 *Fortune* magazine cover, capturing the
entry of Gen-Xers into the workplace

Since the first edition of *Love 'Em or Lose 'Em* in 1999, this group has grown up. They were the new kids on the block then, and now they're solidly at their career midpoint. They are the backbone of every organization's talent planning. They are managers, tenured employees, business owners—and they are busy raising families and contributing to their communities.

There are 66 million of them in the United States, and they are the wellspring of management talent, taking over as the boomers exit the workplace. Scarce and in demand—their numbers are smaller than those of boomers and millennials. They are being hired away from organizations for their expertise and experience.

What They Bring and What They Want

Which of the following ring true for your talented Gen-Xers? Which ring true for you, even if you're in a different age group?

★ **Career portfolio.** This generation takes employability seriously. For them, climbing the corporate ladder was replaced with building a career portfolio that they'll continue to grow. Many have built or are building skill sets that support their need for independence, even as they attain greater levels of responsibility. They can move laterally, stop, and start again; their careers are fluid.

★ **Independence.** Gen-Xers bring an independent approach to their work. They want to clearly understand what's expected. But once expectations are established and deliverables are defined, they need to have space, resources, and the freedom to produce the desired results in their own way and in their own time. Do not micromanage them!

★ **Loyalty, redefined.** While the Xers do not offer blind loyalty to a company, they can be fiercely loyal to a project, a team, a boss they like, the mission of the organization, and, yes, even the organization itself. But that loyalty is based on mutuality. As long as they are being challenged, growing, enjoying the work, and getting recognized for their contributions—and as long as you are getting what you want and need from them—they'll stay. When that partnership weakens or the scales tip to one side, they'll be out of there!

★ **Boundaries.** They also want balance between work and their personal lives. They have boundaries, and they use those boundaries effectively. That doesn't mean they won't put in the occasional all-nighter when it's needed. But don't expect they'll do that for the next 20 years.

★ **Flexibility.** Many feel that one of the greatest gifts of this generation to the rest of us is introducing the expectation of flexibility, freedom, and work-life balance. They don't live to work. They work to live. Find out what kind of freedom they value most and how they can get more of that in their lives. (If you're from an older generation, take a lesson from them on this one!)

Baby Boomers (1946–1964)

Boomers obviously balk at many of the images of slowing down that go with being retired because they imply taking a less important role in the hustling, bustling scheme of things. Boomers want to retain their youth, yes, but even more important, they want to retain their influence.

—Lynne C. Lancaster and David Stillman,
authors of *When Generations Collide*

Will the boomers remain, retire, or return? There are 74 million people in this generation. They are staying in the workforce longer—in numbers not seen before. Proud trendsetters in their youth and at the office, boomers are known for their competitive spirit and hard-working ethic. Their biggest generational conflict arises from being confronted with those in younger generations who do not fit the mold boomers created.

A key to working with them is to develop trust, appreciate their work ethic, and leverage their knowledge. Their focus on personal goals and achievement is a hallmark of their generation. And now, as they approach and pass the traditional retirement age, the boomers have full plates.

Many boomers are part of the "sandwich generation," raising kids and caring for aging parents at the same time. Others, whose children are grown and gone, have more time on their hands and plenty of disposable income. They are helping their kids financially or with childcare. Many are still working full- or part-time, and they are changing the face of retirement.

What They Bring and What They Want

Which of the following ring true for your talented boomers? Which ring true for you, even if you're in a different age group?

★ **Get-it-done attitude.** Boomers have a driven, "get it done at all costs" attitude that has made them phenomenally successful. At the same time, that attitude often conflicts with the three younger generations, who see boomers as having sacrificed everything, including family life, for their own achievement and self-fulfillment. Boomers have been called the "me" generation and accused of being self-absorbed. On the other hand, they see the attitudes of the younger generations as an unwillingness to "pay their dues" and "earn their stripes."

★ **Freedom and flexibility.** Now, they're looking for more balance (thanks, Gen X). They're pondering leaving the workplace, but they don't necessarily intend to stop working. They might want a sabbatical to travel, study abroad, or test-drive retirement. They continue to work for passion, stimulation, a sense of community, and financial need. The question is, what kind of work will they be doing, and can they do that work for you?

★ **Meaning.** They've been looking for meaning in their work and lives since they were 10. Ask what they're passionate about, what some of their current interests are, and how they might blend those passions with their work. Ask, too, what new role they might like to play. They still have plenty of energy and time left to contribute to your team.

★ **Cutting-edge learning.** Keep them on their cutting edge. Teach them. They still want to learn, even the oldest of them. Visit a junior college and notice the silver hair in the world history, pottery, and political science classes. Ask what new thing they'd like to learn this coming year.

Silent Generation (1928–1945), Also Known as "Matures"

Just as the word retirement has outgrown its meaningfulness and should itself be retired, so must the old rules about capturing the ingenuity of this generation.
—Arlene Donovan, Forbes Councils member

Wait—isn't the silent generation gone already? Maybe from your organization. But with increased life expectancy, many people of this generation are still working—in large and small companies, in entrepreneurial ventures, and even in brand-new ways. They are redefining retirement. Many will take advantage of early retirement but will still work. Some will start their own businesses, consult, or work part- or full-time for someone else. Healthy and energetic, others will work well beyond age 75. Still others might even run for president.

Rich with work experience, they built many traditional corporations through their hard work and loyalty. They appreciate and understand the importance of achieving common goals and offer a lasting knowledge legacy. For many reasons, you may want them to stay a little while longer, even in a part-time or advisory capacity.

What They Bring and What They Want

Which of the following ring true for your talented matures? Which ring true for you, even if you're in a different age group?

★ **Respect.** Mine their knowledge. Tell them how much you respect and value what they bring to you, the team, and the organization. Then, really use what they bring! Let them mentor younger workers and pass on their wisdom and knowledge. With more similarities than any other two generations, the combination of a mature and a millennial makes for a great mentoring (and reverse-mentoring) relationship.

X

The company will be in for a real eye-opening as the older work-force is released. No one is teaching the intangibles of the job. You can teach an employee what a pump is and how it works—but not what it sounds like when it's going bad.

—Oil company employee

★ **Legacy.** Matures lead your company, retain your customers, and carry your institutional memories. They are civic minded and helping oriented. And they have a significant knowledge legacy, if only someone will remember to tap into it.

★ **Community service.** Connect them to the community as a way of leveraging their expertise. Ask if they'd like to serve on your organization's community service committee or head up the next charity drive.

★ **Wisdom.** When you start running short on talent or you want someone smart, loyal, hardworking, and connected to your customers, consider hiring a mature, even if only in a part-time position. Many organizations are now partnering with AARP to match job-seeking senior workers with the right employers. These seasoned workers want you to recognize and value their wisdom.

→ TRY THIS

Now that you've read this chapter, ponder and discuss these questions with your team or business unit. Be sure to include representatives from each generation, if possible.

★ What generations are represented among our current and future employees?

★ What does each generation find compelling about our work environment?

★ To be "generation-friendly," what should we stop doing? Start doing? Continue doing?

★ What can we do to bridge generational communication issues in our workplace?

★ What policies, practices, and initiatives should we be looking at through generational lenses?

What did you learn? What will you plan to do more or less of as you take generational differences into account?

If You Manage Managers

Some of the managers you manage think that this chapter is all about pandering. You need to help them see how managing generational differences is a part of strategic leadership. Initiate a conversation with your managers about the workforce they manage. What differences and similarities do they see across generations, and what are the implications for them, as leaders? What benefits could accrue to their departments if they managed all employees with a deeper understanding of generations?

BOTTOM LINE

Remember, you don't have to tie yourself into knots (or worse!) trying to accommodate each generation's individual whims, and you don't have to worry about learning a new set of whims when the next generation comes along. People from different generations are largely alike in what they think, believe, and want from their work life. Once people accept this fact, and make their actions consistent with the principles that apply to working with people of all generations, the gap will be retired.
—Jennifer Deal, author of *Retiring the Generation Gap*

Thank you, Jennifer. We agree.

Learn about generational differences not to separate people but to understand them better and work with them more effectively. Use A-to-Z strategies with all, but keep in mind those that appear to matter most to each generation. And remember that retention is essentially an individual activity. Find out what each of your talented employees wants, regardless of his or her generation.

X

CHAPTER TWENTY-FIVE

Yield

POWER DOWN

Ponder this: Why would you give power away?

Think about being on a highway on-ramp in a busy city, at an intersection with no stop signs, or in a line forming at the movies. When someone says, "No, you go first," with a smile and gesture, you may think how remarkable and rare that action is. To yield is to *give way*.

Similarly, in many workplaces, yielding is all too rare. It could be because managers want to hang on to their power or prestige once they have it. Or perhaps they've never had a manager who empowered them, so they're not sure how it works. They may have learned to micromanage from the boss who never seemed to trust them, looked over their shoulders, and closely inspected every aspect of the work—as they did it.

Exit interviews reveal that micromanagement does not work for most talented employees. Yielding does work. When you yield to your employees, you empower them to think for themselves, to be more creative, more enthusiastic, and probably more productive. Your employees' enthusiasm and sense of value as team members will increase the odds that they will stay engaged and stick around.

Ignore me as needed to get your job done.

—Sign on a vice president's door,
courtesy of Liz Wiseman,
author of *Multipliers*

Why Yield? What's in It for You?

Veronika, a manager in a global drug research and development company, woke up one morning and recognized that 20 percent of her employees were doing 80 percent of the thinking. She was concerned for several reasons:

- *The 80 percent of her employees who weren't really using their creative and intellectual abilities also seemed to be disengaged or just going through the motions at work.*

- *The competition would gain an edge if her company didn't use talent better, get more creative, and stay on the cutting edge.*

- *She and a handful of thinking employees were overstretched and spent much of their time answering questions and meeting with others to solve their problems.*

- *She had lost some talented employees and learned in the exit interviews that they were not being challenged enough and had grown bored.*

Veronika realized that she needed to get at least 80 percent of her people doing the thinking, not 20 percent. And she realized that she was a big part of the problem.

So Veronika did just one thing to yield. She hung a sign on her door that looked like figure 25.1:

What? That's it? End of story? Well, yes, basically. Veronika explained to her employees that she had been underserving and undervaluing them by answering all their questions and giving them step-by-step direction. She admitted to them that she had also robbed the organization of tremendous intellectual and creative capital by giving answers instead of asking questions. So when people came through her open door and asked *their* questions as they always had, she pointed to the sign and asked *them* questions like these:

★   What do you think the problem is?

★   Who do you think should be involved in solving this issue?

★   What are the choices we have?

These questions empowered people to solve problems creatively, to lean on each other instead of on the boss, and to come up with multiple options. Her team's productivity and retention rates surpassed all others' in the organization. Other managers came to her to find out what she was doing to magically inspire such phenomenal results.

→ TRY THIS

Answer these questions yes or no:

★   Is your organization lean and mean, like so many others after years of downsizing?

★   Is your span of control larger than ever, and are the expectations from above constantly increasing your workload and pressure?

★   Do some of your employees seem apathetic or less than eager to show up on Monday mornings?

★   Are many of your employees still waiting to be told what to do every step of the way?

★   Is the competition nipping at your heels?

★   Have you lost any of your talented team members because they were bored or needed a new challenge?

If your answers are no, then either you are already yielding power to your employees or you aren't yet feeling the pressure to do so. If you answered yes to several on the checklist, you have just identified reasons to power down. You must yield to your people to compete successfully. And you must yield to keep your talented employees on your team.

Y

The higher up you go in an organization, the more you need
to let other people be the winners and not make it all about
winning yourself. For bosses, that means being careful about
how you hand out encouragement. If you find yourself saying,
"Great ideas, but . . . ," try cutting your response off at "ideas."
—Marshall Goldsmith, executive coach

Who's Got the Right of Way?

You may be convinced that you could benefit by giving more power to
your employees yet find it difficult to know where to start. The rules
can be fuzzy or hard to remember, just like the road rules that guide
merging into a roundabout or crossing an intersection that has no
stop signs.

In the matter of powering down to your employees, the uncer-
tainty is even greater because *there are no rules.* Your organization
establishes cultural norms and role models, but as an individual manager you have tremendous leeway to give power.

Here are some guidelines for empowering your people:

★ Stop micromanaging. *Stop it.* There—we said it; and it's the
essence of this chapter. The words *micromanager* and *micromanagement* have strong negative connotations. Nobody wants
to be micromanaged or to be considered a micromanager. Yet
very few micromanagers recognize their own leadership style.
Micromanagement kills creativity and stifles learning. Let go.
Stop looking over people's shoulders. Ask them what level of
inspection, critique, or control they *want* you to use as you
manage them. And encourage them to call you out when you
haven't delegated something you should. Negotiate ways to get
quality work done while letting them do it their way.

If I were meant to be controlled, I would have come with a remote.
—Unknown

★ Trust your employees to come up with the answers. Take the
time to encourage new ideas, good and bad. Even if you would
have done something another way, consider the approaches
they create and support them all the way.

A manager at a food manufacturing plant yielded to his assembly-line workers. They developed a schedule and a new team system that boosted production, reduced overhead costs and downtime, and improved recruitment and retention.

★ Manage your reactions when you yield and they crash! Powering down and yielding are sometimes risky, and failures will happen. Instead of punishing, collaborate with your empowered employees to learn from the mistake. Focus on what they could do differently next time around, rather than the rearview mirror approach of what they should have done. A colleague put it this way: "Trust me, then teach me."

A senior manager made a mistake that cost his company $10 million. As he walked into his boss's office, he anticipated anger and most probably a firing. His boss asked him what he had learned from the mistake, and he quickly listed all the things he would do differently next time. Then he waited for the ax to fall. And he waited. Finally, he asked, "Aren't you going to fire me?" The boss answered, "Why would I fire you? I just invested $10 million in your learning."

★ Serve your employees. Be a resource to them. Yielding doesn't mean you take the next exit. Empowerment spells disaster in too many cases where the manager tosses decisions and workloads at his employees and then moves on to bigger things. The "No Answers" approach works only if you are willing to brainstorm with them when they are stumped and to give them guidance and feedback along the way.

★ See them as colleagues, not just subordinates. Show it by occasionally doing work that may seem "beneath you." Working side-by-side with your employees will strengthen your relationships and increase their respect for you.

★ Include everyone. Your team is no doubt diverse and might include those from different generations, cultural or educational backgrounds, communication styles, and more. They will no doubt react differently to this empowerment shift you're making. Yielding might terrify a young employee from a very traditional

Y

patriarchal or hierarchical culture. Ask how you can help this employee take on more decision making, creating, or leading.

★ Listen to and use their ideas. People want a seat at the table. They will tend to withhold their ideas and take less initiative to make improvements when decisions are made without their input. They might be talking, but are you really listening? Do you

- Go into a meeting just to sell your brilliant idea?

- Multitask constantly, checking texts and emails while they talk?

- Glaze over when they bring up a different viewpoint?

- Often respond to an idea or feedback with "Yeah, but . . . " or with automated agreement (the dreaded "corporate nod")?

Effective listening to the ideas, perspectives, and opinions from your diverse team is not only respectful but profoundly productive. If you want to engage and retain your talent, give up the need to be right, *hide your phone* (from you), clear your mind, and really listen.

I had a manager who spent 75 percent of meetings on her iPhone. She would hear snippets of the meeting and make us repeat ourselves constantly. It was so disrespectful and frustrating. We felt unimportant and that our time was not as valuable as others'.
—A colleague of ours

★ Give the spotlight away. This may be the toughest of all. Powering down means sharing the stage and the applause with your team members. Ironically, your stock will go up with your employees as you increasingly give them room to perform (and get credit for) brilliant, creative work.

Your empowered employees will have great ideas or perspective on tasks you may not have asked them to perform. They will put their own signatures on excellence. They may even take your breath away.

If You Manage Managers

We dare you to ask the managers who report to you if you micro-manage them. If they nod their heads, seek specific examples. Ask, "When do I micromanage? What does it look like? Feel like? And what would success look like—you know, if I were perfect?" Now go through the same exercise regarding *their* tendency to micromanage. Having a frank conversation about this topic will put yielding on the radar screen. You and the managers you manage can help each other become even more effective by learning to yield.

BOTTOM LINE

Yielding will increase the odds of retaining your best people. As you give people more power to create, make decisions, and truly affect the success of the team, their job satisfaction (and your odds of keeping them) will go up. At the same time, your ability to compete success-fully and accomplish your business goals will increase. You have phe-nomenal power to yield. Try it and see what happens.

Y

CHAPTER TWENTY-SIX

Zenith
GO FOR IT

Ponder this: How wide is your knowing-doing gap?

Zenith: the point at which something
is the most powerful or successful

We were stuck on Z. Then a client said she was going to a zenith meeting in her company. We said, "What is that?" When she answered, we knew we wanted this chapter to describe how *you* could reach a zenith:

> *It's when an organization regularly brings three or four teams of people together for one purpose: to discuss how, as individual leaders and as an organization, they can continually improve and stretch and grow. They ask each other, "How might we do better?" "Could we reach higher?" "Where's the peak?" And they ask these questions about all aspects of the business—including the people side of the equation. These meetings are future focused, aspirational, and often inspiring. And they yield actionable ideas for continued growth and improvement.*

Aside from organizational zenith meetings, we've seen that amazing leaders (on their own) are always learning, striving to improve, and reaching for a new zenith. In the process they engage and retain talent.

These leaders foster an inclusive climate where differences are not just accepted but embraced. How are you doing in that department? Are you practicing inclusivity, where people of varying cultures, generations, races, or genders can truly thrive? If not, perhaps you are intending to do that.

Sometimes, we just need to close the *knowing-doing* gap.

The Gap between Knowing and Doing

People say that knowledge is power. But we think, "Yes, and." Not until knowledge turns into action is it power. Jeffrey Pfeffer and Robert Sutton literally wrote the book on this topic. They say, "Firms that turn knowledge into action avoid the 'smart talk trap.' Executives must use plans, analysis, meetings, and presentations to inspire deeds—not as substitutes for action."[1]

We all have these gaps. We might *know* we'll learn to play jazz only if we practice, we'll meet the deadline on the new edition of this book only if we write, and we'll have engaged people on our teams only if we notice and thank them. That's the *knowing*. Why then *do* we skip practicing, delay writing, and forget to thank? For some reason, we fail in the *doing* department.

You want your talented people to bring their best to work and to stay—for at least a little while longer. And you know how to make that happen (hopefully more so now, after reading this book). Now, all you have to do is close the gap between *knowing* and *doing*.

Here are some action steps for gap-closing. Highlight one you can do in the next half-hour. Then do it.

★ *Look* at the Retention/Engagement Index (REI) on pages xviii–xix. Answer the questions again and see how your answers compare to the first time you took the quiz. Note the topics that have you wondering or wanting to try something new with your team.

★ *Create* your to-do list. Start with stay interviews for all talented employees on your team. Listen carefully to their answers and note specific action steps that you and they agree on. Read the "Bottom Line" of each chapter to refresh your memory about strategies that work. Remember to include timelines for taking action.

★ *Test-drive* it. Seems obvious. But sometimes, in the context of busy days and business pressures, we just don't get around to trying the new behavior or action. Often, it's easier to stick with a habit—with how we've always done something. This week commit to trying just one thing with one employee.

★ *Get* feedback. How did the test-drive work out? How do you know? The best way to find out is to ask. Go public with your plan; tell people what you're working on and how you're trying to be an even more effective leader. Just telling them might enlist their support.

★ *Choose* again. The popular American TV psychologist Dr. Phil is known to ask, "So how's that working for you?" The question commonly elicits a laugh from the audience. Sometimes you try out a new behavior or approach and then realize that it just doesn't work for you. Don't give up. Try it again in a different way or at a different time. Or think of another action you'll try instead—next week.

★ *Seek* help. You don't have to go it alone. Assuming (hoping) you have a love 'em manager, turn there for mentoring and coaching as you try out new strategies. Human resources partners, colleagues, and workplace coaches can be great resources as well.

The Payoff for Closing the Gap

Everyone says talent is your most important investment. Talent makes or breaks every organization. When people hear that, they nod and say yes, but what are they doing to nurture and grow that investment?

Just knowing you need to listen better, thank often, or mentor more won't help you reach a zenith when it comes to engaging and retaining talent. It's the doing that counts.

Towers Watson stated, "Spiking engagement is one thing; sustaining it is another. In the highest-performing organizations, managers pay attention not only to what increases engagement, but also to what sustains it. In a study of 50 global companies, moving from relatively low levels of engagement to high engagement was found to add more than four percentage points to [the] operating margin. Companies that further bolster and sustain engagement by enhancing well-being and performance support add another 13 points to their operating margins."[2]

Take action. Your efforts to boost engagement will benefit your talented people, you, and your organization.

Z

If You Manage Managers

If you manage people who manage people, you have the task of not only engaging and retaining the talent on *your* team but also helping them do the same with *their* direct reports. Ensure the love 'em message and strategies cascade to all levels of leaders. Model the actions you want them to adopt. Catch them in the act (thanks, Ken Blanchard) of putting those new behaviors into practice.

Invite the managers you manage to join you in a zenith proposition. Ask them how they can continually improve. Follow up with them and measure their progress. *Expect* them to sustain their commitment to talent engagement. Your organization's competitive advantage depends on it.

BOTTOM LINE

You can avoid having the love 'em message and strategies be just another good idea (flavor of the month). Here's how to sustain momentum and continue to build a diverse culture that attracts, engages, and retains the best people.

Evaluate yourself often and commit to continuously improving. Close your knowing-doing gap. Hold yourself and the managers who report to you accountable for building an inclusive workplace that is so productive and fulfilling your talented people will want to stay, create, and make their mark. That's a zenith. We've seen many managers do just that, and we believe you can too.

We wrote *Love 'Em or Lose 'Em* to make your life easier, to help you in a real-time, day-to-day way. We wrote it because you make such an impact on the lives of your workforce. That's an awesome responsibility that deserves all the help and support it can get.

We wish you well.

Conversations That Count

Take Love 'Em Practices Several Steps Forward

Avoid having the love 'em message and strategies be just another good idea. You know: flavor of the month. Ongoing dialogue is one way to sustain momentum and continue to build a culture that attracts, engages, and retains the best people. You probably noticed the punchline in every chapter of this book is to *talk* to your people.

While one-on-one discussions are crucial, conversations in peer groups are equally important. Ongoing dialogue spurs much-needed idea exchanges and cements the organization's dedication to engagement and retention.

On the next pages you'll find a dozen dialogues for managers and another dozen dialogues for human resource and talent management professionals. Go beyond what you find here. Dive into your favorite or most relevant, timely chapters and create your own questions.

An Invitation from Bev and Sharon

We are curious. Which conversations did you have? Tell us where those conversations led you. If you want to dialogue with us about it, please reach out to Bev@BevKaye.com.

Feel free to scan, email, print, copy, and distribute the following pages in preparation for *your* conversations that count.

Enjoy,

Bev and Sharon

A Dozen Dialogues for Managers

Invite a group of colleagues to join you for conversation about engagement and retention. You all have stories, experiences, and perspectives about the topics listed here. Why not share those? You might gain an insight or hear about a strategy for engaging someone on your team. And you might give others some terrific ideas they could implement with their teams. Form chat groups to answer any of the questions below, and remember to add to the list. Choose another chapter from the book and craft your own dialogue questions.

★ **Ask:** Are we conducting regular stay interviews at all levels? How's that going? What are we learning? What creative strategies help talented people get more of what they want here?

★ **Dignity:** How can we make showing respect and valuing diversity part of our DNA? What needs to change to make that happen?

★ **Enrich:** How many of our talented people say they are bored, need a change, or want a promotion? What enrichment activities have worked well with our people?

★ **Family:** In what ways are we family friendly? How do we flex and partner creatively with our talented employees to achieve better balance between work and life?

★ **Hire:** What do we need to do to make sure we're making the best possible hiring choices at all levels? How can we recognize and guard against our own unconscious biases?

★ **Jerk:** What jerklike behaviors have we seen in our own careers with our own managers? What jerklike behaviors are alive and well in our organization? What should we do about that?

★ **Question:** Are we bound by the rules? Which ones no longer make sense? What "silly rules" need to be revisited?

★ **Reward:** What are some of our favorite ways of recognizing all-out effort and work well done? What rewards seem to be working best? Let's create a menu of rewards we can share.

★ **Space:** In what new ways have we been able to give space to our direct reports? To which requests did we say, "No way"? What possible work-arounds have we considered? Where have we given space and then regretted it later?

★ **Understand:** How about a listening challenge for a month? Which listening tips and tricks work best for us? What will we try? In a month we'll ask each other, "What has changed?"

★ **Wellness:** How can we reduce, not increase, employee stress? What can we do more of? Less of? What difference could it make if all managers and employees were healthier?

★ **Yield:** Do any of us accidentally or occasionally micromanage? Why would we do that? And why should we do less of that? What's in it for us—and for them—when we give power away?

A Dozen Dialogues for HR Professionals

Making the love 'em practices come to life demands not only managers who care, but a culture that supports these practices systemically. If you are an HR or talent leader, consider bringing your colleagues together to discuss one or more of these ideas and their implementation. Select more chapters from the book and craft your own dialogue questions.

★ **Ask:** Do we expect managers to ask their employees what will keep them engaged and in our organization? How do we recognize and reward managers for holding these stay interviews?

★ **Buck:** How do we hold managers accountable for engagement and retention? Are they clear about the influence they have in this regard?

★ **Careers:** Do our leaders help talent identify numerous ways to grow their careers? And are managers inclusive, taking differences into account as they support their employees' career development?

★ **Dignity:** Is inclusion a result of engagement, or is engagement a result of inclusion? How are we building a respectful, inclusive culture? What else might we do?

★ **Family:** How free are managers to ease the work-family tug-of- war? How do we know? What else could we be doing to encourage work-life balance?

★ **Jerk:** What are the consequences of jerklike behaviors? Give examples. What happens to the managers in our organization who can't seem to change?

★ **Link:** Are we helping individuals create the networks they need to further their knowledge and increase the quality of their interactions? Give examples.

★ **Numbers:** Do our managers truly understand the cost of loss? Do we? If we do, how might we transfer that knowledge to leaders at all levels?

★ **Question:** Do our managers feel free to push against a policy for the sake of a talented employee's request? What are some examples? Do we sometimes hang onto a rule that has outlived its usefulness?

★ **Reward:** What contributes to or detracts from building a culture of recognition? What unintended biases are we not addressing effectively in our recognition methods?

★ **Space:** There is a trend toward a more open and flexible workplace. How is this true or not true for our organization? How can we better support employees' need for flexibility?

★ **Zenith:** Beyond turnover numbers and engagement surveys, what could we use as measures of success? And how can we help each other, and the managers we support, close the knowing-doing gap?

Notes

Introduction

1. Sally Lauckner, "How Many Small Businesses Are in the U.S.? (and Other Employment Stats)," Fundera, updated April 18, 2020, https://www.fundera.com/blogsmallbusiness-employment-and-growth-statistics.

2. Lou Russell, "Are You a Leader or a Manager? You Need to Be Both," Association for Talent Development, November 16, 2016, https://www.td.org/insights/are-you-a-leader-or-a-manager-you-need-to-be-both.

3. Ed Michaels, Helen Handfield-Jones, and Beth Axelrod, *The War for Talent* (Boston: Harvard Business School Press, 2001).

4. Jeffrey Pfeffer and Robert I. Sutton, *The Knowing-Doing Gap: How Smart Companies Turn Knowledge into Action* (Boston: Harvard Business School Press, 2000).

Chapter 1: Ask

1. Frederick Herzberg, Bernard Mausner, and Barbara Bloch Snyderman, *The Motivation to Work* (New York: Wiley, 1959).

2. Beverly Kaye and Sharon Jordan-Evans, *Hello Stay Interviews, Goodbye Talent Loss: A Manager's Playbook* (Oakland: Berrett-Koehler, 2015).

Chapter 2: Buck

1. Randall Beck and Jim Harter, "Managers Account for 70% of Variance in Employee Engagement," *Gallup Business Journal*, April 21, 2015.

2. Christine Porath, "Half of Employees Don't Feel Respected by Their Bosses," *Harvard Business Review*, November 19, 2014.

3. Jim Clifton and Jim Harter, *It's the Manager: Gallup Finds the Quality of Managers and Team Leaders Is the Single Biggest Factor in Your Organization's Long-Term Success* (New York: Gallup Press, 2019).

4. Amanda Stansell, "Which Workplace Factors Drive Employee Satisfaction around the World?" Glassdoor Economic Research, July 10, 2019, http://www.glassdoor.com/research/employee-satisfaction-drivers/.

5. Beverly Kaye and Sharon Jordan-Evans, *Love It, Don't Leave It: 26 Ways to Get What You Want at Work* (San Francisco: Berrett-Koehler, 2003).

6. Robert I. Sutton, "Why Good Bosses Tune In to Their People," *McKinsey Quarterly*, August 2010.

Chapter 3: Careers

1. Beverly Kaye, Lindy Williams, and Lynn Cowart, *Up Is Not the Only Way: Rethinking Career Mobility* (Oakland: Berrett-Koehler, 2017).

2. Peter F. Drucker, "They're Not Employees, They're People," *Harvard Business Review*, February 2002.

Chapter 4: Dignity

1. Christine Porath, "Half of Employees Don't Feel Respected by Their Bosses," *Harvard Business Review*, November 19, 2014.

2. Willis Towers Watson, "Employers Boosting Efforts to Create Respect and Dignity at Work," press release, February 5, 2020, https://www.willistowerswatson.com/en-US/News/2020/02/employers-boosting-efforts-to-create-respect-and-dignity-at-work.

3. Scott Page, *The Diversity Bonus: How Great Teams Pay Off in the Knowledge Economy* (Princeton, NJ: Princeton University Press, 2019).

4. Patricia C. Pope, CEO and Chief Creative Officer, Pope Consulting, www.popeconsulting.com.

5. Roosevelt Thomas, *Beyond Race and Gender: Unleashing the Power of Your Total Work Force by Managing Diversity* (New York: AMACOM, 1992).

Chapter 5: Enrich

1. Beverly Kaye, Lindy Williams, and Lynn Cowart, *Up Is Not the Only Way: Rethinking Career Mobility* (Oakland: Berrett-Koehler, 2017), 41.

Chapter 7: Goals

1. Beverly Kaye, Lindy Williams, and Lynn Cowart, *Up Is Not the Only Way: Rethinking Career Mobility* (Oakland: Berrett-Koehler, 2017).

Chapter 10: Jerk

1. Christine Porath, *Mastering Civility: A Manifesto for the Workplace* (New York: Grand Central Publishing, 2016).

Chapter 12: Link

1. "Item 10: I Have a Best Friend at Work," *Gallup Business Journal*, May 26, 1999, http://businessjournal.gallup.com/content/511/item-10-best-friend-work.aspx.

Chapter 13: Mentor

1. Daniel Goleman, *Emotional Intelligence: Why It Can Matter More Than IQ*, 10th anniv. ed. (New York: Bantam Books, 2005).

2. Paul G. Stoltz, *Adversity Quotient: Turning Obstacles into Opportunities* (New York: Wiley, 1999).

Chapter 14: Numbers

1. Jim Harter, "Dismal Employee Engagement Is a Sign of Global Mismanagement," *Gallup Blog*, December 17, 2017, https://www.gallup .com/workplace/231668/dismal-employee-engagement-sign-global -mismanagement.aspx.

Chapter 16: Passion

1. Po Bronson, *What Should I Do with My Life? The True Story of People Who Answered the Ultimate Question* (New York: Random House, 2002), 363.

2. Thomas L. Friedman, "It's P.Q. and C.Q. as Much as I.Q.," *New York Times*, January 29, 2013, http://www.nytimes.com/2013/01/30/opinion /friedman-its-pq-and-cq-as-much-as-iq.html.

Chapter 17: Question

1. John C. Lange, *Joshua in a Box*, animated film, Stephen Bosustow Productions (Del Mar, CA: McGraw-HiU Films, 1970).

2. Marilee Adams, *Change Your Questions, Change Your Life: 7 Powerful Tools for Life and Work* (San Francisco: Berrett-Koehler, 2004).

Chapter 18: Reward

1. "Employees in Asia Pacific Want Individual Recognition and Reward," HRM Asia, October 3, 2018, http://hrmasia.com/employees-in-asia -pacific -want-individual-recognition-and-reward/.

Chapter 19: Space

1. "Global Remote Working Data & Statistics," *Merchant Savvy*, updated first quarter 2020, https://www.merchantsavvy.co.uk/remote-working -statistics/.

Chapter 20: Truth

1. Beverly Kaye and Sharon Jordan-Evans, *Hello Stay Interviews, Goodbye Talent Loss: A Manager's Playbook* (Oakland: Berrett-Koehler, 2015).

2. M. Tamra Chandler, with Laura Dowling Grealish, *Feedback (and Other Dirty Words): Why We Fear It, How to Fix It* (Oakland: Berrett-Koehler, 2019), 41.

Chapter 21: Understand

1. Robert B. Catell and Kenny Moore, with Glenn Rifkin, *The CEO and the Monk: One Company's Journey to Profit and Purpose* (Hoboken, NJ: Wiley, 2004), 235.

Chapter 22: Values

1. James M. Kouzes and Barry Z. Posner, *The Leadership Challenge: How to Make Extraordinary Things Happen in Organizations*, 6th ed. (Hoboken, NJ: Wiley, 2017).

2. Amanda Stansell, "Which Workplace Factors Drive Employee Satisfaction around the World?" Glassdoor Economic Research, July 10, 2019, https://www.glassdoor.com/research/employee-satisfaction-drivers/.

Chapter 23: Wellness

1. Geoffrey James, "Stop Working More Than 40 Hours a Week," *Time*, April 26, 2012, http://business.time.com/2012/04/26/stop-working-more-than-40-hours-a-week/.

2. Hans Selye, "The Evolution of the Stress Concept," *American Scientist* 61, no. 6 (November–December 1973): 692–699.

3. "Burn-Out an 'Occupational Phenomenon': International Classification of Diseases," World Health Organization, May 28, 2019, http://www.who.int/mental_health/evidence/burn-out/en.

4. Jennifer Moss, *Unlocking Happiness at Work: How a Data-Driven Happiness Strategy Fuels Purpose, Passion and Performance* (Philadelphia: Kogan Page, 2016).

5. Jena McGregor, "Stanford Professor Says the Workplace Is the Fifth Leading Cause of Death in the U.S.," *Chicago Tribune*, March 23, 2018, https://www.chicagotribune.com/lifestyles/health/ct-workplace-cause-of-death-20180323-story.html.

6. Ben Wigert and Sangeeta Agrawal, "Employee Burnout, Part 1: The 5 Main Causes," Gallup Workplace, July 12, 2018, http://www.gallup.com/workplace/237059/employee-burnout-part-main-causes.aspx.

Chapter 24: X-plore Generations

1. Michael Dimock, "Defining Generations: Where Millennials End and Generation Z Begins," Pew Research Center, January 17, 2019, https://www.pewresearch.org/fact-tank/2019/01/17/where-millennials-end-and-generation-z-begins/.

2. Adapted with permission from the Learning Café, 2013, http://www.thelearningcafe.net.

3. Courtney Vinopal, "Have Helicopter Parents Changed How Companies Attract Employees?" PBS NewsHour, February 17, 2020, https://www.pbs.org/newshour/economy/why-top-companies-are-hosting-take-your-parents-to-work-days.

Chapter 26: Zenith

1. Jeffrey Pfeffer and Robert I. Sutton, *The Knowing-Doing Gap: How Smart Companies Turn Knowledge into Action* (Boston: Harvard Business School Press, 2000).

2. Towers Watson, *Global Workforce Study* (Arlington, VA: Towers Watson, 2012), 8, http://employeeengagement.com/wp-content/uploads/2012/11/2012-Towers-Watson-Global-Workforce-Study.pdf.

Acknowledgments

Each time we have updated this book for a new edition, we have gathered a unique circle of colleagues, friends, and thought leaders in their respective fields. Each time the cast of characters has been slightly different, and each time we agreed we had the best support team yet.

Steve Piersanti has been our editor each time, and each time he continued his warm, sharp, and kind feedback, even when he said, on reading our first edition, "You don't have a book here yet." We both agreed, after every call, that he "nailed it," picking up on every loose end and suggesting great improvements. Thank you, Steve, from the bottom of our hearts! The amazing Berrett-Koehler team has also offered their unflagging innovative ideas and support through all editions.

We also owe a debt of gratitude to Nancy Breuer. She has been our developmental editor for all six editions. We count on her to help us be succinct, engaging, and of course, grammatically correct.

Lindsay Watkins and Lorianne Speaks were incredible support to us, and Bette Krakau was, once again, a research assistant par excellence.

Thanks to the other Sharon and Bev for their brilliant copyediting and typesetting.

Our global facilitators from Career Systems, now Talent Dimensions, kept us current as they received feedback from client organizations. With their internal facilitators, who adapted the material for their organizations, these clients served on the front lines and applied our ideas to a continuously changing workforce.

Specifically, we want to thank Devon Scheef and Diane Thielfoldt, generations experts, and Pat Pope and Judith Katz, thought leaders in diversity and inclusion.

We had wonderful suggestions from many readers including Barry Sagotsky, Ann Kurzenberger, Amanda Chauncey, Michael Thomas, Karen Sistare, Pauline Arneberg, Jeanne Hartley, Becky Willis, Janis Keeley, Louise Keefe, Jana Andrews, Beverly Crowell, Andrew Jones, Jennifer Lodden, Kathryn McKee, KC Simmons, Ann Jordan, Liji Thomas, Wendy Tan, Tracy Rocca, Shelby Earl, Evaan Portillo, and Michele Kennedy. We also appreciate the support of Cile Johnson and Lynn Cowart, from Talent Dimensions. We sincerely apologize if we left anyone out.

We also had our personal cheering squads behind us, led by our husbands, Mike and Barry, and encouraged by our kids, Sharon's grandkids, our friends, and our (late) mascots, Oreo and Roxy.

Bev knows that this work would never have been possible without Sharon's wit, wisdom, and writing skills. Sharon knows that this would not be possible without Bev's fresh eyes, endless supply of great ideas, and amazing colleagues, who bring their knowledge, endorsements, and support for our work. We hope you will find this edition the most useful yet to *you*, our whole reason for writing.

Index

Page references followed by *f* indicate
an illustrated figure; followed by *t* indicate a table.

About the Authors

The authors of this book began their journey together in the late '90s, at the beginning of highly publicized *talent wars*. Employee retention was a relatively new, *hot* topic, as leaders at all levels wondered how they could hang on to their talent while competitors tried to steal them away.

Bev and Sharon wrote this how-to book to help leaders take action and save talent for their teams. They conducted research and published the first edition of *Love 'Em or Lose 'Em* in 1999. They were passionate about the work. Over 20 years and five editions later—they still are.

 **Dr. Beverly Kaye** is recognized internationally as one of the most knowledgeable and practical professionals in the areas of career development and employee engagement and retention.

In 2018, the Association for Talent Development (ATD) honored her with its Lifetime Achievement Award recognizing her advanced knowledge, extensive practice across the talent development field, thought leadership, and contributions to the profession. The Association of Learning Providers (ISA) also honored her with its 2018 Thought Leader Award for her body of work in support of work-related learning and performance. In 2019, Beverly was recognized by the Institute for Management Studies (IMS) with its Lifetime Achievement Award.

Bev's recent books in the career development field include *Up Is Not the Only Way* and *Help Them Grow or Watch Them Go*, which provide overwhelmed managers with a way to blend career conversations into their everyday routine.

As part of her focus on development, Bev recently entrusted Career Systems' legacy to two key members of her leadership team. She supports the rebranded enterprise, Talent Dimensions, which delivers and expertly expands on her thought leadership. Bev is loving the life of a solopreneur again, and she hasn't slowed down yet.

Bev is a transplanted Jersey girl who has made her home in Los Angeles with her husband, Barry, and near her daughters, Lindsey and Jill. For more information, please visit Bev at her company's website, www.BevKaye.com, or email her at Bev@BevKaye.com.

Sharon Jordan-Evans, president of the Jordan Evans Group, is a pioneer in the field of employee engagement and retention. She has worked with the people companies can least afford to lose—their high performers.

As a sought-after keynote speaker, Sharon has worked with Fortune 500 companies such as American Express, Boeing, Disney, Microsoft, Lockheed, Monster, and Universal Studios. She has a master's degree in organization development and is a certified executive coach.

Sharon has also served as a resource for a number of national media, including National Public Radio (NPR), *Business 2.0*, *Chief Executive*, *CIO*, *Harvard Management Update*, *Working Woman*, *Investor's Business Daily*, *BusinessWeek*, and the *Los Angeles Times*.

Born in the Northwest, Sharon grew up in Montana and now lives in Cambria, California, with her husband, Mike. When she's not writing, you'll find her riding a bike or skiing a *well-groomed* slope. She has four grown children and six adorable grandchildren.

Beyond the Book

Keep the Learning Going

The Berrett-Koehler author community practices the love 'em principles in a big way. Authors gather often, support one another, teach one another, and invent together. That mutual support includes recommending each other's excellent work.

Many of the authors listed below have taken a deeper dive into one of our book topics. Here are just a few of the *Love 'Em*–related, BK-authored books you'll want on your shelf.

Ask:

★ *Employee Surveys That Work: Improving Design, Use, and Organizational Impact*—Alec Levenson

Buck:

★ *Be the Boss Everyone Wants to Work For: A Guide for New Leaders*—William Gentry

Career:

★ *Make Talent Your Business: How Exceptional Managers Develop People While Getting Results*—Wendy Axelrod and Jeannie Coyle

★ *Up Is Not the Only Way: Rethinking Career Mobility*—Beverly Kaye, Lindy Williams, and Lynn Cowart

★ *Help Them Grow or Watch Them Go: Career Conversations Organizations Need and Employees Want*—Beverly Kaye and Julie Winkle Giulioni

Dignity:

★ *Inclusive Conversations: Fostering Equity, Empathy, and Belonging across Differences*—Mary-Frances Winters

★ *The 4 Stages of Psychological Safety: Defining the Path to Inclusion and Innovation*—Timothy R. Clark

Enrich:

★ *Life Reimagined: Discovering Your New Life Possibilities*—Richard J. Leider and Alan M. Webber

Family:

★ *The Remote Facilitator's Pocket Guide*—Kirsten Clacey and Jay-Allen Morris

★ *A Great Place to Work For All: Better for Business, Better for People, Better for the World*—Michael C. Bush, CEO, and the Great Place to Work Research Team

Goals:

★ *Going Horizontal: Creating a Non-Hierarchical Organization, One Practice at a Time*—Samantha Slade

★ *Goals! How to Get Everything You Want—Faster Than You Ever Thought Possible*—Brian Tracy

★ *Eat That Frog! 21 Great Ways to Stop Procrastinating and Get More Done in Less Time*—Brian Tracy

Hire:

★ *Hire and Keep the Best People*—Brian Tracy

★ *How to Succeed in Your First Job*—Elwood F. Holton III and Sharon Naquin

Information:

★ *The Discomfort Zone: How Leaders Turn Difficult Conversations into Breakthroughs*—Marcia Reynolds

★ *Breaking the Silence Habit: A Practical Guide to Uncomfortable Conversations in the #MeToo Workplace*—Sarah Beaulieu

Jerk:

★ *Subtle Acts of Exclusion: How to Understand, Identify, and Stop Micro-aggressions*—Tiffany Jana and Michael Baran

★ *Leadership and Self-Deception: Getting Out of the Box*—The Arbinger Institute

Kicks:

★ *301 Ways to Have Fun at Work*—Dave Hemsath and Leslie Yerkes

★ *301 More Ways to Have Fun at Work*—Dave Hemsath

★ *The Power of Having Fun: How Meaningful Breaks Help You Get More Done*—Dave Crenshaw

Link:

★ *How to Be an Inclusive Leader: Your Role in Creating Cultures of Belonging Where Everyone Can Thrive*—Jennifer Brown

★ *Servant Leadership in Action: How You Can Achieve Great Relationships and Results*—Ken Blanchard and Renee Broadwell, editors

Mentor:

★ *Managers as Mentors: Building Partnerships for Learning*— Chip R. Bell and Marshall Goldsmith

★ *Bridging Differences for Better Mentoring: Lean Forward, Learn, Leverage*—Lisa Z. Fain and Lois J. Zachary

Numbers:

★ *Talent Magnet: How to Attract and Keep the Best People*—Mark Miller

Opportunities:

★ *Pacing for Growth: Why Intelligent Restraint Drives Long-Term Success*—Alison Eyring

★ *The Laws of Lifetime Growth: Always Make Your Future Bigger Than Your Past*—Dan Sullivan and Catherine Nomura

★ *Safe Enough to Soar: Accelerating Trust, Inclusion, and Collaboration in the Workplace*—Frederick A. Miller and Judith H. Katz

Passion:

★ *Master Your Motivation: Three Scientific Truths for Achieving Your Goals*—Susan Fowler

★ *The Economics of Higher Purpose: Eight Counterintuitive Steps for Creating a Purpose-Driven Organization*—Robert E. Quinn and Anjan V. Thakor

★ *The Power of Purpose: Find Meaning, Live Longer, Better*—Richard J. Leider

Question:

★ *Change Your Questions, Change Your Life: 12 Powerful Tools for Leadership, Coaching, and Life*—Marilee Adams

★ *Reinventing Talent Management: Principles and Practices for the New World of Work*—Edward E. Lawler III

Reward:

★ *Make Their Day! Employee Recognition That Works*—Cindy Ventrice

Space:

★ *Don't Kill the Bosses! Escaping the Hierarchy Trap*—Samuel A. Culbert and John B. Ullmen

Truth:

★ *Feedback (and Other Dirty Words): Why We Fear It, How to Fix It*—M. Tamra Chandler with Laura Dowling Grealish

Understand:

★ *Creating Introvert-Friendly Workplaces: How to Unleash Everyone's Talent and Performance*—Jennifer B. Kahnweiler

★ *Getting Relationships Right: How to Build Resilience and Thrive in Life, Love, and Work*—Melanie Joy

★ *Erasing Institutional Bias: How to Create Systemic Change for Organizational Inclusion*—Tiffany Jana and Ashley Diaz Mejias

Values:

★ *Whistle While You Work: Heeding Your Life's Calling*—Richard J. Leider and David A. Shapiro

★ *The Critical Few: Energize Your Company's Culture by Choosing What Really Matters*—Jon Katzenbach with James Thomas and Gretchen Anderson

Wellness:

★ *The Resiliency Advantage: Master Change, Thrive under Pressure, and Bounce Back from Setbacks*—Al Siebert

★ *Faster, Fewer, Better Emails: Manage the Volume, Reduce the Stress, Love the Results*—Dianna Booher

X-plore Generations:

★ *Entrepreneurs in Every Generation: How Successful Family Businesses Develop Their Next Leaders*—Allan R. Cohen and Pramodita Sharma

★ *Refire! Don't Retire: Make the Rest of Your Life the Best of Your Life*—Ken Blanchard and Morton Shaevitz

★ *Coaching Up and Down the Generations*—Lisa Haneberg

★ *The Millennial Myth: Transforming Misunderstanding into Workplace Breakthroughs*—Crystal Kadakia

Yield:

★ *Humble Inquiry: The Gentle Art of Asking Instead of Telling*—Edgar H. Schein

★ *Humble Leadership: The Power of Relationships, Openness, and Trust*—Edgar H. Schein and Peter A. Schein

Zenith:

★ *The Purpose Revolution: How Leaders Create Engagement and Competitive Advantage in an Age of Social Good*—John Izzo and Jeff Vanderwielen

★ *Conversations Worth Having: Using Appreciative Inquiry to Fuel Productive and Meaningful Engagement*—Jackie Stavros and Cheri Torres

Guide on the Side—Sage on the Stage

Dr. Beverly Kaye is a bestselling author, dynamic speaker, and internationally recognized authority on career development, employee engagement, and employee retention. She was among the first to recognize the power of this triad on an organization's success. Since her entrepreneurial debut as CEO of Career Systems International (CSI), Bev has used her incisive and inventive thinking to help organizations reduce the costs of talent loss and foster cultures of support. She has refreshed the thinking and behaviors of countless business leaders—a career she continues to this day.

Turning over ownership of CSI, Bev has transitioned from entrepreneur to "solopreneur"—a shift that moves her beyond the vendor category, enables her to spread her wings and her reach, and frees her to interact with clients and colleagues in new and inventive ways previously limited by the demands of managing a full-scale organization. Her new business model is additive, not alternative.

While continuing to share her thought leadership through current and upcoming books and articles, Bev ignites conversations and new thinking as a "Sage on the Stage" keynote speaker. She inspires leadership audiences to "help their employees grow or watch them go," support employee career mobility, and "love 'em or lose 'em."

And in her role as a "Guide on the Side," she breathes new life into career development and employee engagement and retention projects that could better meet the needs of the workforce. Bev consults to talent management leaders, hosts just-in-time discussion groups, facilitates strategic brainstorming sessions, delivers one-on-one career coaching and mentoring, participates on interactive panels for long-term and new clients, and serves on advisory boards.

These are exciting times for progressive business leaders who want to partner with Bev to learn new ways of growing talent.

Learn more about Dr. Beverly Kaye, her publications, and her business offerings at www.bevkaye.com.

Learning Resources

Engaging and retaining talent during any economy depends on providing what employees really want. Research findings from global giants continue to align with our 20+ years of data and analysis from companies large and small. Employees need

★ To have supportive management and a good boss

★ To find opportunities for career growth, learning, and development with challenging and meaningful work

★ To feel valued, included, and respected by their boss and rewarded for their contribution

Talent Dimensions was founded with the belief that the strategic development, inclusion, engagement, and retention of people taps into limitless potential for any organization. It is at this intersection where both individual and organizational performance resides.

The following are a few ways Talent Dimensions helps organizations and leaders develop the skills required to provide what their employees need. All of the Talent Dimensions solutions are available to be delivered face to face, virtually through remote platforms, and digitally.

Supportive Management/Good Boss

No satisfaction—no engagement. Poor engagement—poor productivity. Folks who like what they do usually do it very well. Raising performance through engagement and commitment requires a unique set of skills that managers often lack. Empower employees and they will find more satisfaction at work. Prepare both your managers and employees to have powerful stay conversations and open conversations about workplace satisfaction by using these practical learning solutions:

★ **Love 'Em or Lose 'Em** is a retention and engagement solutions for managers based on the book by the same name.

★ **Engage!** helps employees learn a model of empowerment based on the book *Love It, Don't Leave It.*

★ **Hello Stay Interviews** helps managers fine-tune their stay interview skills based on the book by the same name.

Career Growth, Learning, and Development

Employees with a clear vision of their future are more productive, loyal, and innovative in the work they do. Career development and ongoing learning continue to rank among the top drivers for employee engagement and productivity. Careers are developed one conversation at a time over time. Conversation is one of the most precious and results-driving commodities managers and their employees can share. Talent Dimensions offers these solutions:

★ **CareerPower™ Classic**, a robust solution with a mirrored model for managers and employees, prepares both for career conversations through a lifelong process for managing careers.

★ **GROWhere** is a three-step process delivered as a collaborative and digital solution for managers and employees. Both will learn, practice, apply, and share the development process with learning peers.

★ **Help Them Grow or Watch Them Go**, based on the book by the same name by Beverly Kaye and Julie Winkle Giulioni, offers a simple process for managers to acquire critical career conversation skills.

★ **Up Is Not the Only Way**, based on the book by the same name by Beverly Kaye, Lindy Williams, and Lynn Cowart, provides managers and employees with a practical approach to career mobility.

Feeling Valued, Included, and Recognized

Organizations that focus on building equitable and inclusive cultures where individuals feel valued, recognized, and ultimately included is the silver bullet. This results in higher employee recruitment and retention rates, improved individual and team performance and morale, and increased innovation. Talent Dimensions offers these solutions:

★ **Building Inclusive Teams** gives all managers tools to help foster inclusive behaviors to build an inclusive working environment.

★ **Diversity and Inclusion Means You**, for nonmanagerial employees, is designed to provide additional knowledge and skills for working effectively with all team members and customers in a diverse workplace and marketplace.

★ **Choosing Respect in the Workplace** helps managers and employees build awareness, gain skills, and identify strategies to create and promote a more respectful workplace.

★ **Unconscious Bias: Hidden Perspectives** reveals that unconscious biases can affect hiring, assignments, promotions, evaluations, dismissals, customer service, sales, revenue, profits, and, in healthcare, patient care and safety.

We believe that strategic development, inclusion, engagement, and retention of people tap into limitless potential for any organization. Our simple yet impactful solutions foster meaningful relationships to create an environment where all bring their full selves to work and are more committed to each other's, and the organization's, success.

—Cile Johnson and Lynn Cowart, owners,
www.Talent-Dimensions.com

Also by Beverly Kaye and Julie Winkle Giulioni

Help Them Grow or Watch Them Go

**Career Conversations Organizations Need
and Employees Want, Second Edition**

Frequent, short conversations with employees about themselves, their goals, and the organization are the most powerful tool for driving employee retention, engagement, and productivity. Beverly Kaye and Julie Winkle Giulioni identify three conversations that will increase employees' awareness of their strengths, weaknesses, and interests; point out where their organization and their industry are headed; and help them pull all of that together to create a plan.

Paperback, ISBN 978-1-5230-9750-0
PDF ebook, ISBN 978-1-5230-9751-7
ePub ebook, ISBN 978-1-5230-9752-4
Digital audio, ISBN 978-1-5230-9749-4

Help Them Grow or Watch Them Go Card Deck

**Career Conversations Organizations Need
and Employees Want**

Make career development conversations fun and interactive with the *Help Them Grow or Watch Them Go* card deck. This deck features the most insightful questions leaders worldwide have been asked or wish they had been asked. Use them to assess your development style; engage others; incorporate new, richer conversations into your day-to-day interactions with employees; plan a career conversation with your manager; and more! Career conversations are the single most powerful tool for driving employee retention and engagement, so start talking!

56 cards, ISBN 978-1-5230-9798-2

BK Berrett–Koehler Publishers, Inc.
www.bkconnection.com   **800.929.2929**

Berrett–Koehler
Publishers

Berrett-Koehler is an independent publisher dedicated to an ambitious mission: *Connecting people and ideas to create a world that works for all.*

Our publications span many formats, including print, digital, audio, and video. We also offer online resources, training, and gatherings. And we will continue expanding our products and services to advance our mission.

We believe that the solutions to the world's problems will come from all of us, working at all levels: in our society, in our organizations, and in our own lives. Our publications and resources offer pathways to creating a more just, equitable, and sustainable society. They help people make their organizations more humane, democratic, diverse, and effective (and we don't think there's any contradiction there). And they guide people in creating positive change in their own lives and aligning their personal practices with their aspirations for a better world.

And we strive to practice what we preach through what we call "The BK Way." At the core of this approach is *stewardship,* a deep sense of responsibility to administer the company for the benefit of all of our stakeholder groups, including authors, customers, employees, investors, service providers, sales partners, and the communities and environment around us. Everything we do is built around stewardship and our other core values of *quality, partnership, inclusion,* and *sustainability.*

This is why Berrett-Koehler is the first book publishing company to be both a B Corporation (a rigorous certification) and a benefit corporation (a for-profit legal status), which together require us to adhere to the highest standards for corporate, social, and environmental performance. And it is why we have instituted many pioneering practices (which you can learn about at www.bkconnection.com), including the Berrett-Koehler Constitution, the Bill of Rights and Responsibilities for BK Authors, and our unique Author Days.

We are grateful to our readers, authors, and other friends who are supporting our mission. We ask you to share with us examples of how BK publications and resources are making a difference in your lives, organizations, and communities at www.bkconnection.com/impact.

Dear reader,

Thank you for picking up this book and welcome to the worldwide BK community! You're joining a special group of people who have come together to create positive change in their lives, organizations, and communities.

What's BK all about?

Our mission is to connect people and ideas to create a world that works for all.

Why? Our communities, organizations, and lives get bogged down by old paradigms of self-interest, exclusion, hierarchy, and privilege. But we believe that can change. That's why we seek the leading experts on these challenges—and share their actionable ideas with you.

A welcome gift

To help you get started, we'd like to offer you a **free copy** of one of our bestselling ebooks:

www.bkconnection.com/welcome

When you claim your **free ebook**, you'll also be subscribed to our blog.

Our freshest insights

Access the best new tools and ideas for leaders at all levels on our blog at ideas.bkconnection.com.

Sincerely,

Your friends at Berrett-Koehler

Certified

Corporation